ANDY BULL is a keen walker, journalist and author who has written travel pieces for *The Times*, the *Daily Telegraph*, *The Independent*, the *Mail on Sunday* and *The Tablet*.

He has also written *Pilgrim Pathways: 1-2 day walks on Britain's Ancient Sacred Ways* for Trailblazer. In researching that book, he was surprised to find that the pilgrim route from London to Walsingham, by far the most important path pre-Reformation, was not on maps. When he discovered that the route had died out, he resolved to re-establish it. This book is the result.

Andy has also published two travel books on America: *Coast to Coast* and *Strange Angels*; guides for mountain bikers to The Lake District and The Ridgeway; and *Walking Charles Dickens' Kent*. He has written the local history books *Secret Isle of Wight*; *A-Z of Ealing* and *A-Z of Bexhill on Sea*. He is now working on a further guidebook: *Walking Cornwall's Myths and Legends*.

London to Walsingham Camino – The Pilgrimage Guide

First edition September 2022

Publisher Trailblazer Publications
⊟ trailblazer-guides.com
The Old Manse, Tower Rd, Hindhead, Surrey, GU26 6SU, UK

British Library Cataloguing in Publication Data
A catalogue record for this book is available
from the British Library

ISBN 978-1-912716-31-9

Text © **Andy Bull** 2022
Maps and diagrams © Trailblazer 2022

The right of Andy Bull to be identified as the author
of this work has been asserted by him in accordance
with the Copyright, Designs and Patents Act 1988

Series Editor: Bryn Thomas
Editor: Nicky Slade
Layout: Bryn Thomas   **Cartography**: Nick Hill
Proofreading: Jane Thomas & Bryn Thomas
Index: Jane Thomas

Photographs © Andy Bull all photos except for:
'Waltham Abbey Interior' photos by Poliphilo CCO 1.0 (p53)
© Bryn Thomas (cover and pp164-5)
© Mark Weeks (pp32-3 and p34)

Photos – Cover and this page: Ruined arch of Walsingham Abbey Church (©BT)
Previous page: Through the fields of oilseed-rape after Godwick on Stage 12
Overleaf: Chalk track after Saffron Walden on Stage 5

Important note
Every effort has been made by the author and publisher to ensure that the information
contained herein is as accurate and up to date as possible. However, they are unable to
accept responsibility for any inconvenience, loss or injury sustained by anyone
as a result of the advice and information given in this guide.

Printed in China; print production by D'Print (☎ +65-6581 3832), Singapore

ANDY BULL

LONDON TO WALSINGHAM
CAMINO
THE PILGRIMAGE GUIDE

Contents

Contents

Foreword

I have walked to Walsingham twice, both times with a large group of young people from south London. When I was a curate a group of parishes got together each year and made the journey.

It was the beginning of something important for me. Not only did I discover it was a brilliant way of doing youth work, I discovered the joy and challenge of pilgrimage as it is meant to be, not just arriving, but travelling well. After this, and as an incumbent, I walked with groups of young people to Canterbury, Glastonbury and York, and then eventually, a couple of years ago, I walked the Camino del Norte to Santiago.

Consequently, I am delighted that the route from London to Walsingham is now better established and therefore more available for other pilgrims and also drawn into the network of pilgrimages under the umbrella of the Confraternity of Saint James.

Walsingham is England's Nazareth, the place where we encounter in a fresh and homely way the truth of the incarnation that in Christ has come among us. When we walk to Walsingham this truth is amplified and magnified; we discover that the incarnate God is with us every step of the way.

Stephen Cottrell, Archbishop of York

Author acknowledgements

This project would have been impossible without three pillars of support.

The first is the account of the historic route, *Highway to Walsingham* by Rev Leonard E Whatmore, in which he gathers all available evidence of the medieval route taken to the shrine. That book, published in 1973 by the Pilgrim Bureau at Walsingham, is long out of print, but two very kind people, Isabel Syed, honorary archivist at the Anglican Shrine of Our Lady of Walsingham, and Tim McDonald, archivist of the Catholic Shrine of Our Lady of Walsingham, gave me access to a copy.

The second pillar is that of the footsloggers: the volunteers, members of the Confraternity of St James, who took my initial mapping of possible routes and walked the options, giving me feedback that enabled the best path to be identified. They are: Jim Sollars, Carol and Derek Greening, Sarah Knight, Richard Powell, Tamasine Smith, and Paul McLintic.

Grateful thanks also to Freddy Bowen, general manager of the Confraternity, for supporting the project, along with Wendy Martin for putting me in touch with the volunteers. Also to Peter Doll, Canon Librarian of Norwich Cathedral, and Sarah Friswell at St Edmundsbury Cathedral, Bury St Edmunds for their advice and help.

Standing atop the final pillar is my publisher at Trailblazer, Bryn Thomas, who allowed his heart to rule his head (and wallet) and agreed to publish this book. Much gratitude also to his team, including editor Nicky Slade, cartographer Nick Hill and indexer Jane Thomas.

Acknowledgements

Right: Ruins of the old shrine at Walsingham with the modern shrine in the background, its red-brick tower topped with a golden angel on the weather vane.

The only way is Walsingham

Let me tell you why I think you should walk from London to Walsingham. If you do, you will be journeying to a place that was by far the most important pilgrim shrine in England until Henry VIII outlawed pilgrimage and the veneration of saints in 1538. It was much more popular than Canterbury. Not only that: in the whole of the Christian world it was eclipsed by just three other places: Jerusalem, Rome and Santiago de Compostela.

Those places have enjoyed an unbroken tradition of pilgrimage and veneration stretching back a millennium or more. Not Walsingham. It reverted to being just a village in Norfolk once the pilgrims stopped coming. The road from London ceased to be the most important route in England and faded into obscurity.

For 400 years, no pilgrims walked to Walsingham. Since the 1930s, when both Catholic and Anglican shrines were re-established

Above: Volunteers and members of the Confraternity of St James joined me to help research and re-establish the route in this guidebook.

here, Walsingham has undergone a revival. It draws around 300,000 pilgrims each year, but hardly any of them walk much more than the final Holy Mile, and only a few church and other groups trace the full route from London.

This *London to Walsingham Camino* guidebook is part of an attempt to change that: to re-establish a walking route which, while being as true to the original way as possible, takes account of the modern realities on the ground. A pilgrim path that offers a wonderful long-distance route, on footpaths and quiet lanes, across the glorious east of England. A truly pleasurable and uplifting walking experience.

As I explored the route, I experienced a revelation. I discovered the fundamental difference between simply walking, and walking as a pilgrim. It was as profound as the gulf between speech and song. To travel as a pilgrim made walking a celebration. On my journey I encountered a lost heritage, and experienced an older England: a lost land of saints, faith and observance; of wayside crosses, shrines and chapels.

When I first thought of walking to Walsingham from London, I was surprised to find that no waymarked, long-distance footpath existed that would enable me to do so. While I could easily trace the Pilgrim's Way to Canterbury, I had to refer largely to historical accounts to uncover the path to Walsingham, then apply the ancient way to modern maps.

I also turned to a pilgrim organisation called the Confraternity of St James, which supports British pilgrims who wish to walk to the shrine of St James the Great in Santiago de Compostela, northern Spain. The Spanish have very successfully created a hugely popular and well-supported network of pilgrim routes, including one called the Camino Ingles, or English Camino, which British pilgrims traditionally followed from the Spanish ports of Ferrol or A Coruña to Santiago.

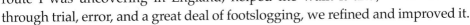

Volunteers, members of the Confraternity who live along the route I was uncovering in England, helped me walk it and, through trial, error, and a great deal of footslogging, we refined and improved it.

While the pilgrim routes that spider Spain on their way to Santiago are lined with hostels (*refugios*), pilgrim churches and shrines, that infrastructure is much patchier on the way to Walsingham. We are doing what we can to compensate for that. A range of churches on the route have agreed to host pilgrim stamps, and you can get a pilgrim passport, a *credencial*, from the Confraternity of St James (🖥 www.csj.org.uk), in which to record your progress. Should you choose to continue your pilgrimage in Spain, you can continue to gather pilgrim stamps along the way, and finally – in Santiago – present your fully-stamped *credencial* to the volunteers at the pilgrim office to prove that you have undertaken the minimum distance to qualify you for a *compostela* (if you state a religious/spiritual motivation) or *certificado* (if you state cultural, sporting or touristic motivation).

In England, the pilgrim hostelries run by religious orders that lined the road to Walsingham were snuffed out along with the monasteries. However, many country inns – a substantial number of which hosted pilgrims – survive, and you will find their details in this guide. We hope in time that a greater network of support and ser-

Below: The scallop shell, traditional symbol of the Camino, on a wall at the Anglican Shrine in Walsingham

vices will grow up along the route, as it has done in recent decades in Spain, with the resurgence of interest in pilgrimage there.

Recognition as a Camino Ingles

This *London to Walsingham Camino* path has been officially recognised by the Spanish pilgrim authorities as a *Camino Ingles* on this side of the Channel, and an official feeder route for those who wish to hop across and walk on to Santiago, as many medieval Walsingham pilgrims will have done. So if you walk at least 25km of the route to Walsingham, and collect pilgrim stamps along the way in a pilgrim passport, it will count for 25km towards the total of 100km you must walk to obtain your *credencial* at the cathedral in Santiago. This then enables you to continue on the shorter version of the Camino Ingles, from A Coruña, rather than the longer one starting at Ferrol.

We also plan to waymark the route from London to Walsingham, to make following it as easy as possible.

For now, however, when you walk to Walsingham you will be something of a pioneer, helping to beat a brand-new path but, at the same time, reclaiming a pilgrimage tradition obliterated almost 500 years ago.

Other routes

In Spain, around 300,000 pilgrims annually walk, cycle or ride the web of ways to Santiago. Once, a similar network of paths existed to Walsingham. One of those routes, from Norwich, has recently been re-established, waymarked and recognised as a *Camino Ingles*. That is down to Revd Dr Peter Doll, Canon Librarian of Norwich Cathedral. Peter plans next to re-establish the route from Kings Lynn. I am liaising with him, and that route will join this one from London in the Norfolk village of Litcham.

There was also an important route from Ely, in Cambridgeshire. If this and the Kings Lynn path were waymarked, pilgrims would have an entire network of Walsingham Camino paths, modelled on that developed so successfully to St James the Great's Shrine at Santiago.

Buen camino!

In the following pages you can read more about the history of Walsingham pilgrimage, what draws pilgrims here, and how to use this guide.

I hope you enjoy your walk and wish you, as they say in Spain *buen camino*!

Why Walsingham?

The importance of Walsingham in medieval England

It is often said that Canterbury was the most important shrine in medieval England. By the time of the Reformation, that was not the case. As Leonard Whatmore writes in his *Highway to Walsingham*: 'By the 16th century offerings at shrines appear to have fallen away. Walsingham, however, retained its popularity.'

He quotes David Knowles, late Regius Professor of Modern History at the University of Cambridge: 'In earlier centuries the body of a saint, real or reputed, or a celebrated relic, had often been a principal source of wealth; by the 16th century this had ceased; two of the most famous shrines of an earlier age, those of St Thomas of Canterbury and of the Holy Blood at Hailes [in Hertfordshire], now received only £36 and £10 respectively. Walsingham alone with an income in offerings of £250, recalled the generosity and faith of the past.'

That sum equates to £240,000 today, according to the Bank of England's inflation calculator.

The medieval road

The road from London to Walsingham was the most important in the country. The Elizabethan chronicler Holinshed put 'The waie from Walsingham to London' first among the 20 main roads in England, which is remarkable for a route, as Leonard Whatmore notes, to a destination that 'is as well off the map as most villages of England, situated in a remote corner of East Anglia, five miles from the sea. Yet the road once thronged with travellers.'

The largest number of pilgrims came from London,

Above: Castle Acre Priory, once a major pilgrimage place on the route to Walsingham is now in ruins and the busy town just a village.

Above: St Edmondsbury Cathedral still dominates Bury St Edmunds

up Roman Ermine Street, a route broadly in line with the modern A10 and A1010 out of the capital, before arcing east along the Icknield Way, a route that may be 3000 years old.

They didn't just come from London. Pilgrims from all over the country converged on Walsingham: from Norwich and Kings Lynn in East Anglia, and from Ely in Cambridgeshire. Those from the Midlands and North converged on Croyland Abbey in Lincolnshire, or came by ship to pick up the route at Kings Lynn. From Kent, and the shrine of Thomas Becket, they crossed the Thames from Gravesend to Tilbury in Essex, approaching via Bury St Edmunds.

Few pilgrims had their sights solely on Walsingham, although it was the holy of holies. Many will have travelled via other important shrines – Bury St Edmunds key among them – as well as Waltham Abbey, Thetford and others. Along the way they will have taken shelter at inns, and the many religious houses on the route, established to give succour to pilgrims.

Then came the Dissolution of the Monasteries, the suppression of shrines, the outlawing of the veneration of saints, and a ban on pilgrimage. This hit Walsingham harder than most other pilgrim destinations. As Whatmore notes: 'Canterbury even without pilgrimage remained a city of ancient and historic importance. Without the shrine Walsingham was nothing, except for the growing of saffron, for which it was noted.'

Above: Saffron crocus on a gravestone in Ugley churchyard.

The Dutch philosopher and Christian scholar Erasmus, who wrote of his pilgrimages to Walsingham and elsewhere, said this Norfolk village was: 'almost entirely sustained by the resort of pilgrimages.' And although April was the most popular month, they came all year round.

Walsingham and the route from London, once thronged with pilgrims, fell into obscurity. While Canterbury has Chaucer to thank for keeping that city's pilgrim tradition alive in the popular consciousness down the centuries, Walsingham had no such advocate, promoter and influencer.

From being one of the most holy places in the Christian world, Walsingham became just a village in Norfolk. And so it remained until the 1930s. But more of that later.

Why pilgrims came to Walsingham

Walsingham was England's Nazareth. A fantastical tale brought pilgrims – kings, queens and commoners alike – to Walsingham in the Middle Ages. In 1061 a Walsingham noblewoman, Lady Richeldis de Faverches, had a vision in which the Virgin Mary transported her soul to Nazareth and showed her the house where the Holy Family once lived, and in which the Annunciation of Archangel Gabriel, foretelling Jesus's birth, occurred. As instructed, she then had a replica of the house built in Walsingham. The Holy House, initially a simple wooden structure, later richly decorated with gold and precious jewels, became a shrine and attracted pilgrims to Walsingham from all over Europe. The shrine was completely destroyed at the time of the Dissolution, but its site is marked in the grounds of the ruined Walsingham Priory (see p186).

The royal path

A string of kings travelled as pilgrims to Walsingham, among them Henry III, who made a dozen visits, the first in 1226; his son Edward I, who matched his tally; and Edward III, a regular supporter of the shrine between 1328 and 1361.

From 1509, Henry VIII gave generous gifts of gold, and made regular payments for a priest to sing before the statue of Our Lady of Walsingham. He came several times, once walking barefoot the final mile. Catherine of Aragon was a regular pilgrim, and Anne Boleyn planned to come, but accounts differ as to whether she made it.

Such royal patronage drove Walsingham's popular appeal.

Our Lady of Walsingham, Marian devotion and St James

Walsingham is dedicated to the Virgin Mary, Christ's mother, and is hence a site of Marian devotion. Mary is venerated more widely than any other saint, and is unique in that, unlike the rest, she was neither a disciple of Jesus nor a Christian martyred for their beliefs.

When we speak of Our Lady of Walsingham we are not talking about some specific version of Mary, simply expressing our belief in Mary's presence in, and protection of, a particular place. So you will find churches called 'Our Lady of ...'. followed by the name of the town in which they stand. Indeed, as you walk the near-180 miles from London you will find many churches dedicated to St

Above: Our Lady of Walsingham figure in the church in Colkirk that takes her name.

Mary, and that number increases the closer you get to Walsingham.

There are also some very significant places along the way dedicated to the patron saint of pilgrims, St James the Great, notably the church at Castle Acre, where many pilgrims spent their last night before reaching Walsingham. At Bury St Edmunds the present cathedral of St Edmundsbury began life as a church dedicated to St James, established by an abbot who, unable to travel to Compostela to venerate the saint, built a church to him instead.

St James is often portrayed carrying the staff and scallop shell that denote his pilgrim status. He is present in several of the churches this route follows, including on the Norman font at St Mary's, in Ware.

Divine guidance

The road to Walsingham was by no means easy to follow for medieval pilgrims. Often, they had to rely on locals to keep them on the true, safe path between chapels where they could gain spiritual nourishment, religious houses where they could shelter, and wayside crosses to point the way through otherwise featureless country. Norfolk in those days was a great Fen, and to stray from the path could easily prove fatal.

It was believed that the Milky Way offered divine guidance to the pilgrim. The Revd Francis Blomefield (1705-52) who published an *Essay towards a topographical history of Norfolk* wrote: 'they believed... that the Galaxies (or what is called in the sky the Milky Way) was appointed by Providence to point out the particular place and residence of the Virgin beyond all places, and was on that account generally in that age called Walsingham Way.'

As Whatmore notes: 'The Galaxy was also appropriated to other pilgrim roads. One of the Turkish names for it was the Hadji's Way, since for them it pointed the way to Mecca. In Italy, in France and in northern Europe it has also been described as St Iago's Way or Jacobstrasse, being supposed to guide pilgrims to the shrine of St James at Compostella.'

The history of pilgrimage in England

Pilgrimage was once universal. Whatmore writes: 'For some it supplied the place of the modern excursion or annual holiday. There were also medical as well as spiritual reasons for making the journey. "Thomas is the best doctor of the deserving sick" was the motto stamped on the pewter flasks which pilgrims bought back as souvenirs from Canterbury. Given the low level of medical knowledge at the time, that was probably right.'

There was also pleasure, even joy, in the journey itself. The various routes leading to Walsingham were named the Walsingham Green Way, or the Palmers Way. Palmers were people on perpetual pilgrimage, named for the palms they carried. Their ranks probably took in both visionary holy men and women, and scroungers exploiting the tradition of offering welcome and sustenance to pilgrims.

Looking back through the centuries, pilgrimage was popular in Saxon times. From the 6th century, Celtic saints and itinerant holy men came from Ireland and Wales, spreading the gospel and, on occasion, travelling on to Santiago, Rome and Jerusalem. Among ordinary people there were few set routes or itineraries, and many pilgrimages were very local. By the 10th century, however, key shrines became of national importance.

The first saint to gain a national following was Cuthbert, a 7th century monk and abbot of Lindisfarne whose shrine is in Durham Cathedral. Royal devotion helped his cause. It may be that Cuthbert's remains were moved to Durham in around 1018-20, during the reign of King Canute, who as an early pilgrim gave great support to the monks at Durham. He also venerated St Edmund, the East Anglian king killed by heathen Danish invaders in 869, and pilgrimage to his shrine at Bury St Edmunds gained a national dimension during Canute's reign.

Other key figures who attracted pilgrims from across the country include Edward the Confessor, at Westminster Abbey. English pilgrimage gained an international dimension in 1170 when Thomas Becket, archbishop of Canterbury and 'turbulent priest', was mur-

Above: The Martyrdom, the shrine to St Thomas Becket in Canterbury Cathedral

dered by knights loyal to Henry II, with whom Becket was in a power struggle.

But, as we have seen, the appeal of this first genuinely English clerical martyr became eclipsed, in the 16th century, by the appeal of Our Lady of Walsingham.

Walsingham today

In the 1930s, both Anglican and Catholic shrines were re-established at Walsingham, and you can read more about this development in Stage 13. The Catholic shrine is in the Slipper Chapel, a mile from the Holy House, where pilgrims would leave their shoes and continue barefoot. The Anglican shrine is in the centre of the village, alongside the ruins of Walsingham Priory, where the Holy House stood. There are both official and unofficial pilgrim hostelries in Walsingham, and the village once again feels almost entirely sustained by pilgrimage.

How this London to Walsingham route was chosen

I have drawn on a range of historic sources to identify the most likely route from London to Walsingham. Leonard Whatmore did a wonderful job in the 1970s of collating all the available evidence and outlining the medieval route. However, he did not walk it, nor apply it to modern maps. He drew heavily on the work of Francis Blomefield, mentioned earlier, and other sources to suggest a route that ran north from London on Ermine Street to Waltham Abbey and Ware, both pilgrim destinations in themselves.

Today, that walk through the North London suburbs is not a pleasant one. However, shift a mile or so east and you find a wonderful alternative, via the Lee Valley. Here you can walk from London to Waltham Abbey and Ware, barely putting foot to tarmac. And, as Revd Peter Smith, rector of Waltham Abbey Church, assured me when I discussed this stretch of the route with him, the river was used by monks at Waltham, and by some pilgrims.

Above: The route passes Audley End House, near Saffron Walden

From Ware, Whatmore's route arcs east via Hare St and Barkway to take in Newmarket and Mildenhall. I have walked it and, while the first half is pleasant enough, the five miles before Newmarket are an unrelenting grind along the verge of very fast A roads, there being no footpaths following that section of the route, and hence no easy way to shadow it. Also, with one or two exceptions, the pilgrim points along the way no longer exist, and hence the sustenance that the medieval pilgrim would have gained is no longer available to us today.

So I have chosen to take a slightly shallower arc from Ware, which takes in a string of pilgrim points that are still extant, and which offers a far finer walk. Key among them is Bury St Edmunds. It also takes in Saffron Walden, where Walden Abbey has morphed into Audley End House, Bishop's Stortford, and Thetford, another place that exerted a powerful draw to medieval pilgrims.

From Thetford I re-join the route outlined by Whatmore, still fine walking country today, with a little juggling to avoid restricted military zones, and the A roads criss-crossing Norfolk. I take in Brandon, where pilgrims from Ely, and from destinations in the Midlands and the North would have joined the main route; and Castle Acre, generally considered to be the last stop for many London pilgrims before Walsingham.

Our hopes for the future

Mapping the *London to Walsingham Camino* route, having it officially recognised as a Camino Ingles, and producing this guide form just the first stage in our efforts to make the route fully accessible to as many people as possible. Eventually, in conjunction with the relevant local authorities and with the permission of landowners, we hope to waymark the entire route.

As the route develops...

As additional facilities become available to pilgrims, it may be necessary to make adjustments to the route. Such changes will be made to the online resources available to all who buy this book, and in future editions of it.

THE LANGHAM MADONNA – IS THIS THE TRUE ORIGINAL?

In the basement of London's Victoria and Albert Museum is a very battered and time-worn wooden statue. According to its label, it is 'The Virgin and Child Probably 1220-30'. The rest of the description is equally vague: '...probably an altar figure... very few survive... removed or destroyed during the Reformation.' The V&A bought it, in 1925, for just £2/10s (£2.50) at a London auction. But two historians have a theory that this is none other than the original statue of Our Lady of Walsingham, the most sacred image of medieval England, which stood in the Holy House at Walsingham Priory and which, rather than being seized and burned by Cromwell's men as history records, was spirited away.

Michael Rear and Frances Young presented their evidence in an article in *The Catholic Herald.* They believe it was hidden by local Catholic loyalists led by the Revd John Grigby, priest of Langham, a village six miles from Walsingham. Grigby certainly had form. In 1537 he was arrested for his part in the 'Walsingham Conspiracy', an unsuccessful plot by armed locals to defend the shrine against destruction. The mastermind, Ralph Rogerson, and other conspirators were hanged, drawn and quartered, some in Martyrs Field at Walsingham (see p185). Grigby, however, was allowed to return to his ministry at Langham.

Among his parishioners were the Calthorpe family of Langham Hall, who were *recusants*, secret Catholics. The theory is that the Langham Madonna was hidden in their house, and inherited in 1555 by another recusant family, the Rookwoods.The Rookwoods hid at least one other Marian image: Our Lady of Euston. It was discovered, buried in a hayrick, in 1578 while Elizabeth I was visiting them. If the statue of Our Lady of Walsingham was also hidden, then Elizabeth's men must have missed it.

The only confirmed image of Our Lady of Walsingham is a priory seal, which Fr Alfred Hope Patten, who established the Anglican Shrine at Walsingham, used as a model for a much larger carved wooden statue to be placed in the shrine. It is this likeness that is used in most other representations of Our Lady of Walsingham.

That image bears a striking likeness to the battered statue in the V&A. The position of the two figures is identical, and the Christ child has his right arm raised across Mary's breast just as on the seal. So, could this really be the original, or is it a mere 12th-century copy? Those who hope the theory is correct point out that there is no eyewitness account of the Walsingham statue's destruction, and there are conflicting reports as to where it was burned: one saying in a pyre at Smithfield, the other in the court of Cromwell's house in Chelsea.

We may never know. But, should the theory ever be proven correct, that £2.50 was money extremely well spent by the V&A.

Overview – The 13 stages

1 London to Waltham Abbey
17.7 miles/28.5km

From the pilgrim church of St Magnus the Martyr, with its shrine to Our Lady of Walsingham, to the abbey of the Holy Cross, burial place of Harold, the king slain at the Battle of Hastings. This is a waterside walk, following the Thames Path downriver to Limehouse Basin, then joining the towpath alongside the Regent's Canal, the Hertford Union Canal, and the River Lee Navigation. The walk upriver from here is through a vibrant, regenerating swathe of the city past Hackney Wick and on via Lea Bridge and the nature reserves of the Hackney Marshes to Tottenham Locks.

The increasingly rural second half of the stage takes you out of the city and on through open country, via Stonebridge Lock and Rammey Marsh Lock to Waltham Abbey.

2 Waltham Abbey to Ware
13.2 miles/21.2km
(*30.9 miles/49.7km* from London)

From the church of Waltham's great Augustinian abbey to the medieval wayside memorial that gave Waltham Cross its name, then along the River Lee valley to the ancient pilgrim town of Ware.

The first half of this stage, to the village of Broxbourne, is through the peaceful, wildlife-rich, watery world of the River Lee Country Park, a 1000-acre nature reserve. From Broxbourne the New River, actually a 17th century aqueduct built to supply London with drinking water, takes you to Rye House, childhood home of Henry VIII's sixth wife, Katherine Parr. Then it's another wonderful walk, bordered by flooded gravel pits and nature reserves, on a combination of New River and River Lee Navigation – via the beautiful village of Great Amwell, with its 11th century church – all the way to Ware.

3 Ware to Stansted Mountfitchet *16.4 miles/26.4km*
(*47.3miles/76.1km* from London)

From Ware – its High St known in medieval times as Walsingham Way – via the tranquil River Ash valley to the delightful village of Much Hadham, with its former Bishop's Palace and church adorned with works by Henry Moore, a local resident.

Much of this stage follows the Hertfordshire Way long-distance path over the rolling hills to Bishop's Stortford and then up the Stort valley to Stansted Mountfitchet. Along the way are three very traditional English churches with soaring Hertfordshire Spike spires and a pair of delightfully unexpected Italian Romanesque and Renaissance-inspired gems.

4 Stansted Mountfitchet to Saffron Walden 14.2 miles/22.9km
(61.5 miles/99km from London)

Through the north Essex countryside via Audley End – a palace in all but name, built on the site of a monastery dedicated to the pilgrims' patron, St James – and on to the town with the loveliest church in the county.

The stage follows stretches of the Saffron Trail and Harcamlow Way over chalk downs and through a string of peaceful villages with fine Norman churches to reach Saffron Walden, whose splendid church sails like a great stone ship above the hill-top town.

5 Saffron Walden to Withersfield 13.8 miles/22.3km
(75.3miles/121.3km from London)

This stage runs deep into the heart of the English countryside, following the Harcamlow Way from the town that took its name from the saffron crocus, over the Essex hills to Cambridgeshire, and on into Suffolk.

There is a strong Marian theme along the way, with three churches dedicated to St Mary, one with a wonderful bronze depicting her at the moment of the Annunciation, plus the Guildhall of St Mary, once a place of sanctuary for the poor. There is also a wide range of other sites with a religious significance, from a turf labyrinth to a sacred Roman tumuli burial site.

6 Withersfield to Stansfield 12.2 miles/19.7km
(87.5 miles/141km from London)

This stage, far from towns and with few villages, offers a meditative amble through bucolic Suffolk countryside, beneath vast, ever-changing skies. Between the points of habitation, which offer lovely medieval churches and welcoming inns, the Camino route follows green ways and quiet lanes in a landscape that is quintessentially English. Along the way is a village where madder, the rare and valuable red dye, was produced, and Chipley Abbey Farm, site of a medieval priory.

7 Stansfield to Bury St Edmunds 12.2 miles/19.7km
(99.7 miles/160.7km from London)

The route crosses the highest point in Suffolk on the way to the great pilgrim town of Bury St Edmunds, home to England's one-time patron saint, and half-way to Walsingham.

The route takes in a string of quiet villages, among them Hawkedon, where splinters of the shattered English pilgrim tradition survive in the church, St Mary's. Here I find a barely legible portrayal of St James, and a scallop shell in a fragment of stained glass. I walk on over the heights to Whepstead, where St Petronilla's, a unique dedication in England, recalls the leper hospital of St Petronilla in Bury St Edmunds.

8 Bury St Edmunds to Thetford 16.3 miles/26.3km
(116miles/187km from London)

Bury St Edmunds is a holy town, one of the most important pilgrim destinations in England. Here they venerate St Edmund, a 10th century king who – before George – was patron saint of England. The town's cathedral was dedicated to St James the Great of Compostela, patron saint of pilgrims, by an abbot unable to make the journey to Santiago.

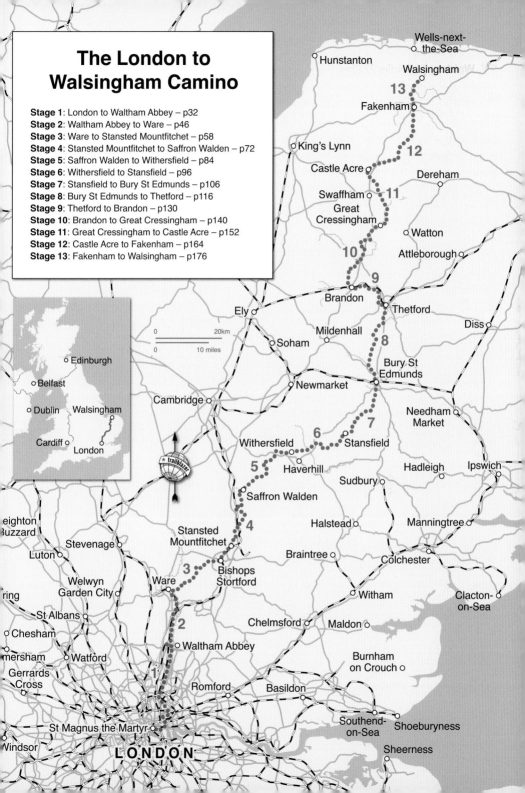

The London to Walsingham Camino

There follows a riverside and forest ramble – via the River Lark and St Edmund Way – to Thetford, the next key medieval pilgrim staging post on the road to Walsingham. In contrast to these two busy market towns, the path that links them touches just two villages – Culford and Barnham – and is otherwise through one of the most remote regions I encounter. Today's walk provides a calming contrast to the bustle that bookends it.

9 Thetford to Brandon
10.5 miles/16.9km
(126.5 miles/203.9km from London)

The next staging post for medieval pilgrims headed for Walsingham was Thetford where, at the riverside Priory of Our Lady, a statue of the Virgin Mary was said to perform miracles. Henry VIII visited – and prayed at – this place, which had a particularly personal importance for him. For it contained the tomb of his illegitimate

THE STAGES

Stage No	From/To	Distance (Miles/Km)	Cumulative Total
1	London to Waltham Abbey	17.7 miles/28.5km	17.7 miles/28.5km
2	Waltham Abbey to Ware	13.2 miles/21.2km	30.9 miles/49.7km
3	Ware to Stansted Mountfitchet	16.4 miles/26.4km	47.3miles/76.1km
4	Stansted Mountfitchet to Saffron Walden	14.2 miles/22.9km	61.5 miles/99km
5	Saffron Walden to Withersfield	13.8 miles/22.3km	75.3miles/121.3km
6	Withersfield to Stansfield	12.2 miles/19.7km	87.5 miles/141km
7	Stansfield to Bury St Edmunds	12.2 miles/19.7km	99.7 miles/160.7km
8	Bury St Edmunds to Thetford	16.3 miles/26.3km	116miles/187km
9	Thetford to Brandon	10.5 miles/16.9km	126.5 miles/203.9km
10	Brandon to Great Cressingham	15.6 miles/25.1km	142.1 miles/229km
11	Great Cressingham to Castle Acre	13.7 miles/22.1km	155.8 miles/251.1km
12	Castle Acre to Fakenham	15.9 miles/25.6km	171.7miles/276.7km
13	Fakenham to Walsingham	6.2 miles/10km	177.9miles/286.7km

*Note: Times include only the actual walking time.

son, Henry FitzRoy, who died of consumption at the age of 17. Because of that, this was one of the last monasteries seized by Henry.

From Thetford Priory, a walk alongside the River Little Ouse leads via the site of St Helen's Oratory and still-existing holy well, and a little gem of a forest church, to the pilgrim town of Brandon.

10 Brandon to Great Cressingham
15.6 miles/25.1km
(*142.1 miles/229km* from London)

I discover a surviving stretch of the Walsingham Way, and a string of medieval pilgrim places, as I trace the ancient route from the site of the Augustinian house at Brandon, and hunt out the remains of a great stone cross on a hill beyond Weeting that guided pilgrims onward.

A former pilgrim hostelry at Ickburgh

AT A GLANCE

Walking Time*	Total Ascent	Level of Difficulty	Types of Terrain
6hrs 10mins	239m/784ft	Moderate terrain, challenging distance	Almost entirely flat, city pavements in early section, then gravel and sealed towpaths
4hrs 30mins	141m/462ft	Easy	Mostly flat, mainly well-maintained towpaths
5hrs 50mins	337m/1105ft	Moderate	Rolling countryside
5hrs	263m/862ft	Easy	Gently rolling hills, walking on footpaths and quiet lanes
5hrs	316m/1037ft	Moderate	Footpaths
4hrs 20mins	328m/1076ft	Easy	Gently rolling hills
4hrs 15mins	178.5m/568ft	Easy/Moderate	Footpaths and quiet lanes
5hrs 30mins	133.4m/437ft	Moderate	Mainly riverside and sandy forest tracks; almost entirely flat
3hrs 40mins	123m/403ft	Easy	Riverside and forest paths
5hrs 10mins	141m/462ft	Moderate	Mainly forest tracks and quiet lanes; almost completely flat
4 hrs 50 mins	234m/767ft	Easy/moderate	Following the Peddars Way on quiet lanes and footpaths; gently undulating country
5 hrs 30 mins	218m/715ft	Moderate	Following footpaths and quiet lanes over very flat country
2hrs 15 mins	115m/378ft	Easy	Mainly quiet country lanes over gently undulating countryside

Allow an extra 20-40% to allow for stops.

and the site of a wayside chapel at Hilborough line the route, in a walk that combines forest stretches and country lanes with lively villages and good inns.

11 Great Cressingham to Castle Acre 13.7 miles/22.1km

(155.8 miles/251.1km from London)

The anticipation heightens as I join the ancient Peddars Way – in the footsteps of Katherine of Aragon – to walk via an isolated hill-top church rescued from satanists at Houghton on the Hill to Castle Acre, the last stop for many medieval pilgrims before Walsingham.

The ancient path I follow hugs the heights above the Wissey valley, guiding me to insular villages and unexpected treasure-houses such as the round-tower church at South Pickenham with its organ case designed by AWN Pugin, and St George's at South Acre with wonderful poppy-head pew ends depicting a snail, a frog, a dolphin and an otter with a fish in its mouth.

12 Castle Acre to Fakenham 15.9 miles/25.6km

(171.7miles/276.7km from London)

Castle Acre combines two gems: the substantial remains of the great priory where many pilgrims spent their last night before Walsingham, and a church dedicated to St James the Great.

The evidence of pilgrimage-past grows ever stronger on this, the penultimate stage of the Walsingham Camino. On my way via quiet lanes and lovely villages to

Fakenham, I encounter several more very solid survivors from medieval times, including another important priory beside the River Nar at Litcham, where pilgrims from King's Lynn would have joined the route, and a thousand-year-old round tower church at East Lexham that is among the oldest in the country.

13 Fakenham to Walsingham 6.2 miles/10km

(177.9miles/286.7km from London)

This short stage covers the final, glorious approach to England's Nazareth, passing through sacred ground where kings including Henry VIII walked barefoot for the final approach.

It starts at Fakenham's church of St Peter and St Paul, where many saints were venerated, and proceeds through quiet lanes and footpaths to the village of East Barsham. It is here, at All Saints, that many pilgrims prepared themselves for the final passage to the Holy House, and it is also where, at the orange brick manor house, Henry VIII stayed.

I continue over the fields to the Slipper Chapel, a survivor from medieval times which now houses the Catholic Shrine of Our Lady of Walsingham, where pilgrims traditionally removed their shoes to continue barefoot to the Holy House.

In Walsingham itself, I encounter Walsingham Abbey's ruins, where the Holy House stood, and the Anglican shrine, which contains a 1930s replica of the original shrine.

How to use this book

The information for each stage comes from two sources: this book and downloads accessible only to readers of this book from a web address given with each stage.

In the pages that follow, I recount my experience of walking the 13 stages; a descriptive overview designed to give you an idea of what each stage holds and to inspire you to walk it. When you are ready to walk a particular stage, go to the website page which has been created specifically to hold the downloads you'll find useful for navigation. The web page address is given in the practical information box of each stage in this book.

Downloadable practical information

On the website you'll find three files for each numbered walk:

● **.pdf file for paper-based walking instructions** This printable pdf file is a tabulated, step-by-step description, designed to be used in conjunction with the paper Ordnance Survey (OS) Explorer map listed in the book.

● **.gpx file for GPS route** If you have a smartphone with GPS capability (most modern phones have this) or a GPS unit (such as a Garmin) you can upload the relevant gpx file into the app used on it and follow that as you walk. Each gpx file was recorded as I walked a given route, so should keep you exactly on the route, which will appear on your screen as a solid line.

If you are using the gpx file on your phone you'll need an app to load it into. I use the Ordnance Survey's app but there are several other apps that use OS mapping. If you download the route to your phone, you can follow it even if your phone loses its signal at some point.

● **.kml file for use with GoogleEarth** The GPS file is also supplied in this format. You can import it into GoogleEarth on your computer and make A4-sized screenshots of each birds-eye section of the walk which you could print out.

Note that you don't need all of these files to do the walks. If you prefer just using paper maps simply print the pdf file to use with your OS map.

How to use this book

How to download the files from the website

These files on the internet do not appear on our public website as they are intended only for readers of this book. It is most important that you type the url directly into your browser. If you try to access it using a search engine (such as Google) it won't show up.

If, for example, you wish to get the files for Stage 5 you'll have seen in the practical information box the following:

● **Directions & GPS** 505.pdf, 505.gpx, 505.kml at ⌨ https://trailblazer-guides.com/press

Open your browser and type: https://trailblazer-guides.com/press into the browser to replace whichever website address the browser usually opens with. This will take you directly to the list of files on our website. Click on the required files to download them.

As explained above, there are three files for each stage: the **printable pdf file** with the walking and map directions, the **gpx file** if you're using gps navigation and the **kml file** if you want to see the route on GoogleEarth.

Planning your itinerary

The 13 stages

The route is divided into 13 stages, averaging 14 miles each. Keen walkers will find they can accomplish each in around five to six hours. The whole 177.9 mile pilgrimage could be accomplished by a fit walker in a fortnight or less. But maybe you want to walk for fewer miles each day, or just at weekends, or on odd days when you have the time and energy.

Halving the daily walk or setting your own itinerary

For those who prefer to tackle a much shorter daily mileage, each stage can be divided roughly in half, meaning the route can be accomplished in 26 bites averaging seven miles each.

If you prefer to fashion your own itinerary and perhaps vary the distance you walk each day, we've listed details on where you can obtain refreshments and accommodation in many other towns and villages along the way. That means you can stop and start at numerous points within each stage.

Pilgrim points, stamps and passports

The route passes many pilgrim points – priories, cathedrals and churches – and you will find details on visiting them. A number of them have pilgrim stamps, and the Confraternity of St James has produced a pilgrim passport, a *credencial*, in which you can record your journey (🖳 www.csj.org.uk).

Transport to and from the stages　[see Public Transport map overleaf]

Transport information is given below and in the Practical Information sections of each stage to enable you to reach the start of each stage, if needed. There are also various public transport apps you may find useful, but we've found Rome2Rio (🖳 rome2rio.com) great for working out the best ways to and from a walk via public transport of all varieties.

If there are two or more of you on the walk and two cars you can of course park one at the end of a stage and then drive to the start, leaving the other car there to be collected later.

RAIL ROUTES & OPERATORS

Greater Anglia (🖳 greateranglia.co.uk)
● London Liverpool St to Cambridge via Tottenham Hale, Cheshunt, Broxbourne, Bishops Stortford, Stansted Mountfitchet, Newport & Audley End, daily 2/hr
● London Liverpool St to Stratford via Hackney Wick, daily 7/hr, Sun 4/hr
● London Liverpool St to Hertford East via Tottenham Hale, Brimsdown, Enfield Lock, Waltham Cross, Cheshunt, Broxbourne, Rye House, St Margarets, Ware daily 2/hr
● London Liverpool St to Ipswich via Bury St Edmunds daily 2/hr
● London Liverpool St (change at Cambridge) to Norwich via Brandon, Thetford daily 2/hr, Sun 1/hr

BUS ROUTES & OPERATORS

Bus route operators
● Arriva (🖳 arrivabus.co.uk/connecting-communities/herts-and-essex)
● Central Connect (🖳 centralconnect.info)
● Coach Services (🖳 coachservicesltd.com)
● First: Norfolk & Suffolk (🖳 firstbus.co.uk)
● Go To Town community minibuses (🖳 gtt-online.co.uk, ☎ 01553-776971)
● Hedingham & Chambers (🖳 hedinghamandchambers.co.uk)
● Lynxbus (🖳 lynxbus.co.uk)
● Stagecoach East (🖳 stagecoachbus.com)　　　　　　　　　　*(cont'd overleaf)*

BUS ROUTES & OPERATORS (*cont'd*)

- Star Cabs (⌨ startraveluk.com, ☎ 01440 712712)
- Stephensons of Essex (⌨ stephensonsofessex.com)
- The Voluntary Network community minibuses (⌨ thevoluntarynetwork.org/community-transport) Pre-booking essential: ☎ 01638-664304, lines open Mon-Fri 8am-4pm, or email fhbookings@thevoluntarynetwork.org at least 1 day in advance). Routes vary depending on demand.

Bus routes

excel A/B/C Peterborough to Norfolk via Wisbech, Kings Lynn & Swaffham, Mon-Sat 2/hr, Sun 1/hr (First: Norfolk & Suffolk)

SE1 Newmarket to Haverhill via Withersfield, Barnham, Great Wratting, Hundon, Stansfield, Culford & Rede, Mon-Sat 1/hr. (The Voluntary Network)

X29 Yellow Line Fakenham to Norwich, Mon-Sat 1/hr (First: Norfolk & Suffolk)

12 Swaffham to North Pickenham, Mon-Fri 2/day (Go To Town)

13/13A Haverhill to Cambridge via Horseheath, Mon-Sat 1/hr (Stagecoach East)

14/15 Haverhill to Bury St Edmunds via Great Wratting, Mon-Fri 1/hr, Sat 5/day (Stephensons of Essex)

32 Swaffham Flexibus via Litcham & Castle Acre, Mon-Fri 1-2/day (Go To Town)

36 Coaster Fakenham to Kings Lynn via East Barsham & Walsingham Mon-Sat 1/hr, Sun 5/day (Lynxbus)

40 Thetford to Kings Lynn via Mundford Mon-Fri 4/day OR via Brandon Mon-Fri 5/day, Sat 1/day NB: Check timetable for stops as routes vary. (Coach Services)

59/60 Audley End to Haverhill via Saffron Walden Mon-Fri 1/hr, Sat 5/day (Stephensons of Essex)

84/86 Bury St Ed to Brandon via Barnham, Thetford Mon-Sat 2/hr (Coach Services)

200/201 Thetford to Mildenhall via Brandon Mon-Fri 1/hr, Sat 6/day & Santon Downham Mon-Fri 4/day, Sat 3/day (Coach Services)

301 Saffron Walden to Bishop's Stortford via Audley End, Newport, Stansted Mountfitchet Mon-Sat 9/day (Stephensons of Essex)

310 Waltham Cross to Hertford via Cheshunt, Broxbourne, St Margarets, Great Amwell & Ware, Mon-Sat 3/hr, Sun 1/hr (Arriva)

332 Thetford to Bury St Edmunds via Culford, Mon-Sat 4/day (Coach Services)

351 Hertford to Bishop's Stortford via Ware, Great Amwell, St Margarets, Hunsdon, Widford, Much Hadham, Mon-Fri 10/day, Sat 4/day (Central Connect)

351 Great Bradley to Haverhill via Withersfield, Mon-Fri 2/day (Star Cabs)

374 Clare to Bury St Ed via Whepstead, Mon-Sat 3-4/day (Hedingham & Chambers)

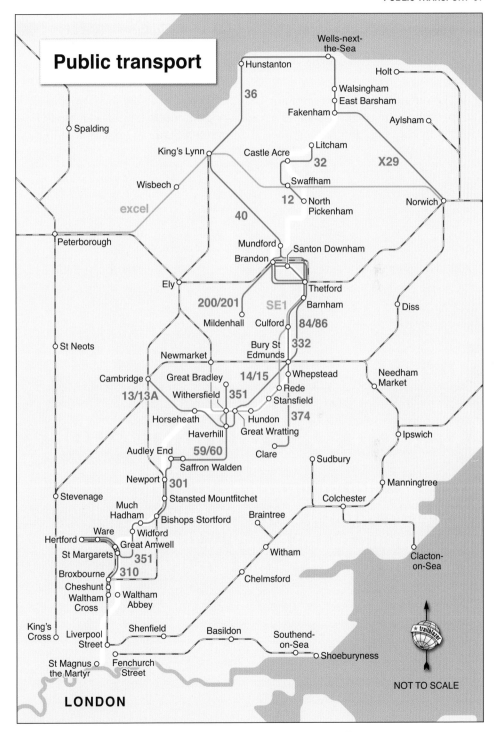

Public transport

NOT TO SCALE

1

London to Waltham Abbey

From the pilgrim church of St Magnus the Martyr with its shrine to Our Lady of Walsingham, to the abbey of the Holy Cross where King Harold is buried

I am standing on the left bank of the Thames beside London Bridge. To the south is Southwark, where Chaucer's pilgrims began their journey to Canterbury and the tomb of the murdered St Thomas Becket. If I were to walk a little way south down Southwark Bridge Road I would find a galleried inn, the George, which is very similar to the Tabard, from which Chaucer's twenty-one departed.

But I am going to turn my back on all that and, with a band of fellow pilgrims, walk north on a very different pilgrimage. One that was a far more popular destination than Canterbury in the 16th century, but which – lacking a Chaucer to fix it in the popular consciousness down the centuries – has been eclipsed. My pilgrimage is to Walsingham, and a shrine dedicated not to a slain priest, but to Mary, Christ's mother. Pre-Reformation, the importance and popularity of the shrine of Our Lady of Walsingham was outshone only by Jerusalem, Rome and Santiago de Compostela.

The bridge used by the medieval pilgrims has long gone, and its replacement spans the Thames 100 yards upstream of the original. Much has changed in the city, but I can just make out the spire of **St Magnus the Martyr** on the north bank, enclosed by modern office towers. The old road passed right before the church door, and pilgrims – for both Canterbury and Walsingham – would stop off there. Half way across the old bridge was a chapel dedicated to St Thomas, administered from St Magnus. It appears in stained glass in the church. There too is a detailed scale model of the medieval bridge.

But there is something else that makes St Magnus the Martyr special. It holds a shrine to Our Lady of Walsingham. Today, this church marks the **official start point for the revived London to Walsingham Camino**, and I am very fortunate that its rector, Fr Philip Warner, has agreed to send us on our way with the traditional prayers before his church's shrine.

From here, we will walk downstream beside the Thames to another place with a powerful link with past pilgrims: **The Royal Foundation of St Katharine** at Limehouse. It has been caring for its local community, and pilgrims, since 1147, and today it offers shelter and succour to those embarking on the Walsingham Camino.

From Limehouse we shall walk alongside the Regent's Canal, and then up the Lea Valley. After 10 miles, my fellow pilgrims will leave me, and I shall forge on to **Waltham Abbey**, the next key place of medieval pilgrimage on the route to Walsingham. And, in something of a minor modern miracle, my feet will barely touch tarmac all the way.

The Royal Foundation of St Katharine © Mark Weeks

PRACTICAL INFORMATION

Route overview   17.7 miles (28.5km)

From St Magnus the Martyr, at the northern end of London Bridge in Lower Thames St, you pick up the Thames Path, diverging from it after **2.7 miles** for the Royal Foundation of St Katharine. You then walk past Limehouse Basin to join, after a further **400 yds**, the towpath alongside the Regent's Canal. You leave the canal at Victoria Park, after **1.5 miles**, walking through the park and then along the Hertford Union Canal, reaching the River Lee Navigation in a further **1.3 miles**.

You follow this waterway, reaching Lea Bridge after **1.9 miles**, and Tottenham Locks, where **the stage can be most easily divided**, after **2.2 miles**.

In another **0.7 miles** you reach Stonebridge Lock, where there is a café. Further refreshment points occur near Enfield Lock, after **5.4 miles**, and at Rammey Marsh Lock, after **0.6miles**. Waltham Abbey is reached in a further **0.9 miles**.

Public transport options

Setting off from central London means that this whole first stage is easily accessible by overground and/or underground **train** services. The starting point at St Magnus the Martyr is 200yds from Monument Underground station while the end of the stage, at Waltham Abbey, is 1 mile west of Waltham Cross railway station. Between the two there are stations at or near Limehouse, Victoria Park, Lea Bridge, Clapton, Tottenham Hale, Seven Sisters, Stonebridge Lock, Enfield Lock and Rammey Marsh. See also public transport map and table pp29-31.

Where to eat or stay along the way

● **Limehouse** (after 2.7 miles/4.3km) **Stay** at *Royal Foundation of St Katharine* (☎ 0300-111 1147, 🖳 rfsk.org.uk, 2 Butcher Row) our accommodation partner. **Eat** in their adjacent, eclectic, open-air *Yurt Café* (open daily 9am-9pm). Get to the start from nearby **Limehouse station**.

● **Victoria Park** (after 4.6 miles/7.4km) Pause for **refreshments** at *Park Café* (Tue-Fri 9.30am-3.30pm, Sat-Sun 9.30am-4pm, Mon closed).

A guest room at St Katherine's
© Mark Weeks

● **Terrain** Almost entirely flat, city pavements in early section, then gravel and sealed towpaths
● **Difficulty** Moderate in terms of terrain, challenging in terms of distance
● **Time** 6hrs 10mins actual walking time
● **Total ascent** 239m/784ft
● **Maps** OS Explorer *173 London North; 174 Epping Forest & Lee Valley*
● **GPX route file & directions*** 501.pdf, 501.gpx, 501.kml at 🖳 https://trailblazer-guides.com/press * See pp27-8 for more information on downloads

● **Lea Bridge** (after 7.7 miles/12.5km) Stop for **lunch** in the large, tented garden at the *Princess of Wales* pub (☎ 0208-533 3463, 🖳 princessofwalesclapton.co.uk, 146 Lea Bridge; open 11am-11pm, food 11am-10pm).

● **Clapton** (after 8.4 miles/ 13.5km) Another **lunch** option is Fullers' *Anchor and Hope* pub (☎ 0208-806 1730, 🖳 anchor-and-hope-clapton.co.uk, 15 High Hill Ferry; open Mon-Fri 1pm-11pm , Sat noon-11pm, Sun noon-10.30pm, **food** Sat-Sun noon-9pm) which has riverside tables.

● **Tottenham Hale** (after 9.4 miles/15.1km) If dividing up this stage, **stay** at *Premier Inn* (☎ 0333-003 8101, 🖳 premierinn.com; Station Rd), a reliable chain hotel 400yds from the route.

● **Seven Sisters** (after 9.4 miles/15.1km, then 1 mile/1.6km off route) Leave the route at Markfield Park to **stay** at *The Fountain* (☎ 0208-802 0433, 🖳 fountainhotellondon.com, 125 W Green Rd) a Victorian hotel with **pub** and Japanese **restaurant**.

● **Stonebridge Lock** (after 10.7 miles /17.2km) Stop for **coffee** at *Waterside Café* (Wed-Sun 10am-3pm, Watermead Way), a community café with toilets.

● **Enfield Lock** (after 16 miles/25.9km) The *Greyhound* (☎ 01992-711271, 🖳 mcmullens.co.uk/greyhoundenfield, Ordnance Rd; Mon-Fri 11am-10pm, Sat 11am-10pm, Sun noon-10pm) is a traditional **pub**.

● **Rammey Marsh Lock** (after 16.7 miles/26.9km) *Narrowboat Café* (🖳 facebook.com/TheNarrowboatCafe, Rammey Marsh; daily 7am-5pm) is a licensed full menu **café** on a canal boat.

● **Waltham Abbey** The most convenient place to **stay** is *Premier Inn* (☎ 0333-003 8101, 🖳 premierinn.com; Sewardstone Rd) 0.6mile/1km from the route. Alternatively, Waltham Abbey Town Council has a list of

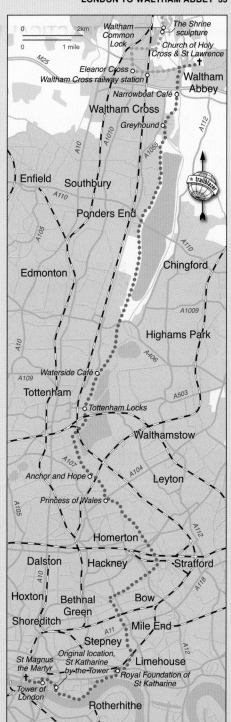

B&Bs on its website (💻 walthamabbey-tc.gov.uk/business). There is a good choice of places to **eat** including *The Gatehouse Café* (☎ 07971-800727, 2-4 Highbridge St; Mon, Tue, Thur & Fri 8am-5pm, Sat & Sun 9am-5pm) for all-day breakfast, daily hot specials and sandwiches; the *Welsh Harp* (☎ 01992-711113, 💻 mcmullens.co.uk/welsh-harp, Market Sq; Mon-Thur 11am-11pm, Fri-Sat 11am-midnight, Sun 11am-10.30pm) for good pub grub; or *Royal Artisan Bakery* (tel 01992-700841, 💻 facebook.com/royalartisan .essex, 11 Sun St; daily 9am-5pm) for great cakes and coffee.

Services
● **Waltham Abbey** For picnic supplies there's Tesco **supermarket** on Sewardstone Rd (Mon-Sat 8am-11pm, Sun 11am-5pm) and Lidl on Cartersfield Rd (Mon-Sat 8am-10pm, Sun 10am-4pm). Should you need a **laundrette** try Pearl Launderette (☎ 01992-650650, 45 High St; daily 8am-7pm).

PILGRIMAGE HIGHLIGHTS

● *St Magnus the Martyr* (💻 stmagnusmartyr.org.uk, Lower Thames St; open Tue-Fri 10am-3pm, Sun 10.30am-1.30pm, closed Mon & Sat; **Services:** Sun 10.30am Office for the Fraternity of Our Lady de Salve Regina, Sun 11am Solemn High Mass, Tue, Wed & Fri 12.30pm Low Mass). For organised groups, contact them to discuss the possibility of a welcome and prayers from Fr Philip Warner. **Pilgrim stamp in church.**
● *Royal Foundation of St Katharine* (☎ 0300-111 1147, 💻 rfsk.org.uk, 2 Butcher Row). Pilgrims receive a warm welcome – contact them to let them know you are coming. **Pilgrim stamp in reception**.
See Stage 2, p50, for pilgrimage highlights in Waltham Abbey.

Beginning the Pilgrimage

Mud. Cormorants. Fog. The Thames is silent, low and still: hovering at that point between ebb and flow. Downriver, beyond the washing-line of cormorants – perched along a beam, wings hung out to dry – Tower Bridge frames a block of fog. The battleship-grey *HMS Belfast* (**below**) dissolves in the murk. One thing the fog does is truncate the towers that soar into the sky around St Magnus. Once, this church was the tallest building on the north bank of the Thames, together with the Memorial to the Great Fire, whose golden orb peers through the buildings just up Fish St.

Today, with cloud billowing just above the apex of St Magnus's Wren spire (**right**), and swallowing anything that has the audacity to rise above it, the

church regains something of its old and rightful prominence, despite being squeezed half to death by the 20th century blocks that crowd it. I go in, to begin my pilgrimage to Walsingham.

St Magnus the Martyr

We, a little band of pilgrim brothers and sisters, stand before the Shrine to Our Lady of Walsingham while Fr Philip Warner sends us on our way with the prayers from the itinerary of the Walsingham Manual, a blessing for those beginning a journey. He first reads the parable of the Good Samaritan, commenting, as he finishes:

'Whenever I do the prayers for the beginning of a pilgrimage I do wonder whether that doesn't scare some pilgrims off, the thought that they might fall

The pilgrim chapel on the old London Bridge is commemorated in glass (above) at St Magnus's, while a plaque (**below**) records the church's location beside that bridge.

among robbers between here and Walsingham, but it is a timely reminder that pilgrimage was not always a safe journey to make, especially if you were going abroad. Say you were going to Jerusalem. No guarantee that you would get there or that you would get home but one made the pilgrimage in faith and trust.'

Then come the prayers:

'Heavenly Father, protector of all who trust in you, you led your people in safety through the desert and brought them to a land of plenty. Guide these, your faithful people, who begin

their journey today. Fill them with your spirit of love, preserve them from all harm and bring them in safety to their destination. We ask this in Christ our Lord'.

And then a second prayer:

'May our Lord Jesus Christ be with you to defend you, within you to keep you, before you to lead you, behind you to guard you, above you to bless you. We ask this of Him who lives and reigns with the Father and the Holy Spirit for ever and ever.

'And may our Lady of Walsingham, St Mag-

ST MAGNUS THE MARTYR'S PILGRIM HISTORY

St Magnus the Martyr's connection to Walsingham pilgrimage, severed at the Reformation, was re-established when a new rector, who followed the Anglo-Catholic tradition, came to the parish in 1921. Henry Joy Fynes-Clinton was great friends with Alfred Hope Patten, who established the Anglican Shrine of Our Lady at Walsingham. Fynes-Clinton became a patron there, and organised pilgrimages starting at this church.

The shrine to Our Lady of Walsingham at St Magnus's

He also created a shrine to Our Lady of Walsingham in St Magnus's, as part of extensive work to beautify the building, transforming it into a baroque church in the Catholic tradition. Among the church's admirers was the poet T.S. Eliot who writes, in *The Wasteland*, of its 'inexplicable splendour of Ionian white and gold'.

The bond between St Magnus and Walsingham was a profound one. In 1928, Fynes-Clinton presented a votive candle to the shrine at Walsingham 'in token of our common Devotion and the mutual sympathy and prayers that are, we hope, a growing bond between the peaceful country shrine and the church in the heart of the hurrying City, from the Altar of which the Pilgrimages regularly start.'

nus, St James, and all the saints pray for you, and may almighty God bless you, the Father, the Son and the Holy Spirit.'

Then he sprinkles us with Holy Water and, now fully protected, we are on our way.

St Magnus the Martyr to Limehouse

The fog is lifting as we leave St Magnus, the Thames Path guiding us downriver, looping around the Tower of London, tunnelling beneath Tower Bridge Rd, then funnelling us through a narrow gap between towering wharves to reach an expanse of water. This is St Katharine Docks, today

harbouring expensive motorboats and alfresco brunchers, but for six centuries the home to The Royal Foundation of St Katharine, a remarkable institution that has been caring for the poor and welcoming pilgrims since 1147.

All that was up-ended in 1825 when the religious house, its chapel, cloister, guesthouse, and the homes of 3000 people were destroyed and the 23-acre site dug out to create a dock: two linked basins accessed via a lock from the Thames.

It was an extraordinary act of wanton and pointless vandalism: the dock created was

HISTORY OF ST KATHARINE'S AND ITS PATRON SAINT

St Katharine

St Katharine's was founded in 1147 by Queen Matilda, wife of King Stephen, in memory of two of her children, who died in infancy. It was a centre for worship and hospitality, and cared for the old, infirm, the poor and children. It once had a choir to rival that of St Paul's.

The foundation has continued under the protection of queens in an unbroken line right down to the present day. Eleanor of Castile, wife of Edward I, and Philippa of Hainault, wife of Edward III, were particularly committed to the foundation. Philippa and Edward's statues guard the entrance to the present chapel.

At the Reformation, the foundation escaped dissolution, perhaps because it was under the protection of Catherine of Aragon, who remained patron even after her divorce from Henry VIII. Instead it was re-established as a Protestant institution.

Through its dedication to St Catherine of Alexandria it is wedded to pilgrimage. It was the Knights of St Catherine who once guarded the road to Nazareth and the Holy House, a replica of which is at the centre of Walsingham devotion.

St Catherine of Alexandria was one of the most popular saints in medieval Europe. She was martyred by the Romans in the 4th century, and her symbol is the spiked wheel – the Catherine Wheel – on which she was tortured. Edward the Confessor was among those who made the difficult pilgrimage to Mount Sinai, bringing back a vial of the healing oil said to issue from her body, and placing it in Westminster Abbey.

too small to take large ships, and was among the first to be abandoned as the London Docks lost their *raison d'etre*, and fell into dereliction.

But, while St Katharine's was displaced, it survived in a sort of exile from its East End heartland, in Regent's Park. After the Second World War it found a new home, just downriver from here, and is once again an oasis of calm for its local community, and a place of sanctuary, sustenance and accommodation for pilgrims walking the Walsingham Camino. More of that in a moment.

Wapping and Limehouse

We walk the gangplank between the two basins and reach Wapping, passing through the yellow-brick canyon of immaculately restored warehouses and on to Shadwell, the Thames Path darting now and then between river and road. From the riverbank we look over at the Shard, a great glass-spired cathedral to commerce, soaring above Hay's Wharf and London Bridge Hospital.

Through Wapping and Limehouse the old waterfront pubs turn their backs to the street, their beer-flushed faces to the river,

Above: Immaculately restored Wapping warehouses (**left**) and the Bascule Bridge in Shadwell Basin (**right**).

from which the sailors could climb straight from boat to bar. I count off The Town of Ramsgate, the Captain Kidd, and the Prospect of Whitby on the way to Shadwell Basin, where the oxblood-red Bascule Bridge bares to the world the same mechanism that powers Tower Bridge's lifting roadway, but which there is sheathed in stone. The great counterweight mechanism stands, ready to raise the road in a salute to any boat that wishes to pass beneath it.

After King Edward Memorial Park, a sustained riverside stretch draws us to the start of that fallopian loop in the river seen beneath the credits on *EastEnders*. Here, a prospect opens up of the modern city downriver. The fog has cleared to reveal the cluster of towers at Canary Wharf beneath a soot-black sky that threatens a pilgrim-drenching downpour. But the rain holds off as, just before Limehouse Basin, we turn north up Narrow St for Butchers Row, and the second truly powerful place for pilgrims on this walk.

The Royal Foundation of St Katharine

We navigate the snarling traffic of the Commercial Rd to enter a remarkable sanctuary: the modern incarnation of The Royal Foundation of St Katharine. It stands on the site of the former church of St James Ratcliffe,

which was destroyed in the Blitz that devastated so much of the East End during the Second World War. Today its chapel, guest house, restaurant and meeting rooms form a protective ring around a green space which has the feel of an open cloister.

This is truly an oasis in the city; the thrum and grind of London almost completely shut out. Chaplain Carol Rider

Below: Pilgrims setting out from the Royal Foundation of St Katharine.

gives us a tour, starting in the chapel which was added in the 1950s. Not all was lost when St Katharine's original chapel beside the Tower was destroyed. Some of the choir stalls, with their intricately carved misericords featuring mythical beasts, were rescued, and grace the new chapel.

In the floor, a marble compass has at the centre a piece of orange marble from St Katharine's Monastery on Mount Sinai, the oldest surviving monastery in the world. Around it is written: 'We do not come to God by navigation but by love.'

Next comes the former vicarage, a lovely 18th century merchant's house, where the walls of the lounge are filled with the original painted murals of bucolic southern European scenes. We walk on from St Katharine's through its Yurt Café, passing beneath the railway arches at Limehouse DLR station and skirting Limehouse Basin.

The Regent's Canal to Victoria Park

At Limehouse Basin we forsake the Thames for the Regent's Canal and walk alongside the run of locks that takes it gently uphill through Mile End to Hackney. We are walking through the heart of the East End, but the combination of parkland to our right almost all the way, and the still waters to our left, make this feel like a far more rural stretch than it is.

At Victoria Park we turn east, emerging to walk through the green expanse of what is London's oldest public park, before dropping down to another towpath, this one along the Hertford Union Canal, which takes us to the River Lee* Navigation.

OTHER PILGRIM POINTS IN LONDON

If you have time in the capital before starting your pilgrimage, you might like to explore the following:
- **Catholic Church of the Immaculate Conception,** better known as **Farm St** (☎ 020-74937811, 🖥 farmstreet.org.uk; see website for opening and mass times; 114 Mount St W1K 3AH) welcomes Catholic pilgrims setting out for Walsingham.
- Shrine of the Martyrs at **Tyburn Convent** (☎ 0207-7237262, 🖥 tyburnconvent .org.uk/martyrs-shrine; guided tours 3.30pm but call to confirm, 8-9 Hyde Park Pl, W2 2LJ) This was London's gallows, where saints and others were executed.
- **Westminster Abbey** (☎ 0207-222 5152, 🖥 westminster-abbey.org, SW1P 3PA) is a royal church offering daily services for all and a World Heritage Site with over a thousand years of history.
- **St Paul's Cathedral** (🖥 stpauls.co.uk, EC4M 8AD), designed by Sir Christopher Wren, is one of the most iconic sights of London.
- **Tower of London** (🖥 hrp.org.uk/tower-of-london; Sun & Mon 10am-5.30pm, Tue-Sat 9am-5.30pm, EC3N 4AB) See the holy marks cut into the walls by those about to be martyred, and the burial place of two murdered saints, two queens and Thomas Cromwell.

Above: There are working boats on the River Lee* Navigation.

The River Lee Navigation via Hackney Wick to Lea Bridge

The original pilgrim route up Roman Ermine Street, now the A10 and A1010, is clogged with traffic and smothered by swathes of London suburbia. Yet, barely a mile east of it is this fine waterway through open country: a green artery that the Walsingham Camino route follows all the way to Waltham Abbey, and on to Ware.

The Lea Valley is also a region of great renaissance. At the point where we join it, the London Stadium, built for the 2012 Olympics and now home to West Ham United, is just over to our right, with Anish Kapoor's Orbit sculpture, an *avant-garde* helter-skelter, peeping above it.

There are many floating enterprises: cafés, bars and vendors of street – or rather river – food. And houseboats, hundreds of them. With their stumpy chimneys puffing wood smoke, their roofs lined with mini allotments, sprawling bicycles and solar panels, they create a great linear city stretching all the way to Ponders End, and sporadically on to Waltham Abbey.

There are working boats, too: Lynx No 39 of the South Midland Water Transport Limited chugs past, its hold brimming with Calor gas and smokeless coal.

As we pass through Hackney Wick and on towards Lea Bridge, the grimy walls and bridges have been enlivened with art too bright and vibrant to be described as graffiti. And, all the while, the expanse of Hackney Marshes to our right gives me the sense of walking along the very rim of London. I'm not, of course, the conurbation spreads out on all sides, but the Lee River Navigation offers what feels like a timeless escape route. There is wildlife, too: a coot tramps down its mid-river nest on grey-rubber feet that would suit a much bigger bird; a pair of swans spread their wings around their gaggle of six cygnets resting on the bank.

Lea Bridge to Tottenham Hale

We have been walking along the right (east) bank of the navigation, but just before Lea Bridge we cross a footbridge to the left. At around the eight-mile mark

---

* Lea or Lee? You'll see this river and valley spelt with an 'a' or an 'e' but the convention seems to be that it's 'Lea' when referring to the natural river and its valley and 'Lee' for the widened navigation part of the river and its valley.

Above: Cross the river at Enfield Lock

there are a couple of pubs for lunch: The *Princess of Wales* at Lea Bridge, just before the A104 passes over the waterway, and the *Anchor and Hope* at Upper Clapton, where Walthamstow Marshes takes on the role of offering greenery to my right.

If you would like to divide this first stage of your pilgrimage into two, Tottenham Lock is a good place to do so. Tottenham Hale's rail and tube station, and accommodation, are close at hand. Indeed, this is where my pilgrim brothers and sisters depart, while I press on solo for Waltham Abbey. For much of my pilgrimage to Walsingham I shall walk alone, but others will join me for stretches, making for a perfect mix of companionship and solitude.

Tottenham Lock to Enfield Lock

Life on the river is conducted at walking pace. As I pass the lock at Tottenham a working boat is released and we chug alongside each other. The bargee sees the size of my pack and asks where I'm headed. When I tell him 'Walsingham, in Norfolk' he cups his hand behind his ear, as if he hasn't heard me right, raises his eyebrows and opens his mouth. So, as we head on in tandem alongside a string of vast reservoirs stretching almost all the

way to Waltham, I explain about re-establishing the Camino route. He wishes me luck but says he will only travel where the water takes him.

The towpath, which has so far been busy with runners, dogwalkers and cyclists, is quiet out here, and I have the place to myself as the river takes me on across Tottenham Marshes. At Stonebridge Lock, with six miles to go to Waltham, the *Waterside Café* looks very inviting, so I stop for an afternoon snack to see me through my final stretch.

At Pickett's Lock an interpretation board urges me to look out for otters beneath the slogan: 'Otters – the sign of a healthy river.' It illustrates their footprints, poo and riverbank homes, or holts. I don't see otters, but the river is clean enough to show its bottom.

Wildlife is all around me now. At Ponders End the pylons alongside are covered with starlings, packed so densely onto every strut, cable and wire that it looks as if they've been sprayed on as a feathery coat. Later there'll be a murmuration but for now they are just chattering among themselves.

Enfield Lock to Waltham Abbey

Waltham is only a couple of miles away when I reach Enfield Lock, where the path crosses over from right to left, and continues along a high bank that protects the row of houses down below the water level. There is a pub here too, *The Greyhound*, the last before Waltham.

At Rammey Marsh Lock there is the final refreshment point: the *Narrowboat Café*, which offers a full service to river folk, including showers and a laundry, plus breakfast, lunch and dinner. Not long after it, I pass beneath the many lanes of the M25, and know that I have definitely left Greater London behind.

A mile further and I leave the towpath where the A121, Station Rd, runs over the water. Turning right here I can see Waltham Abbey Church in the distance, leading me on to my destination for tonight. As Churchill might have put it, I

Above: Waltham Abbey; the end of Stage 1

have reached the end of the beginning of my pilgrim journey.

Beside the Lee as it passes by Warwick Reservoir

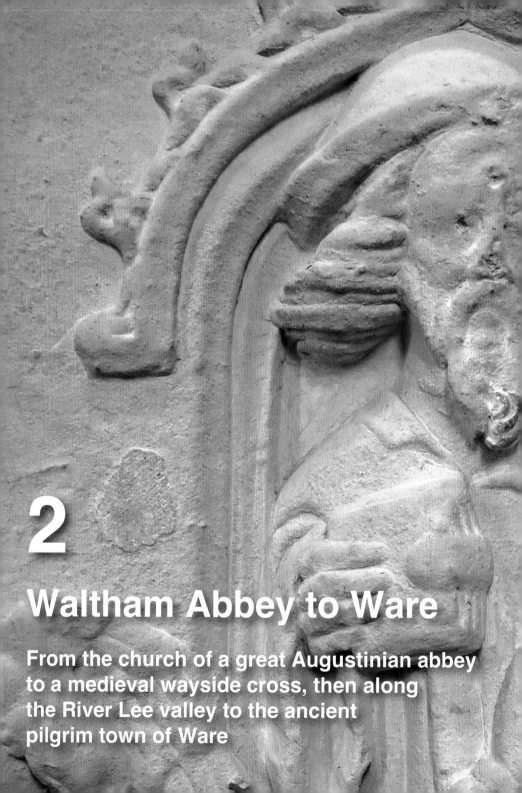

2

Waltham Abbey to Ware

From the church of a great Augustinian abbey to a medieval wayside cross, then along the River Lee valley to the ancient pilgrim town of Ware

At Waltham Abbey I reach the first major place of worship for medieval Walsingham pilgrims after leaving London. They were drawn to this abbey because of a remarkable 10th century Holy Cross, an object of veneration for a string of kings including Edward the Confessor, Harold, and Henry VIII. This, the Montacute Cross, was lost at the Dissolution but, little more than a mile further on, a second medieval cross survives. It is the 13th century Eleanor Cross, and pilgrims paused to honour the romantic story behind it.

From Waltham Cross, riverside trails through reed-marsh and watermeadow will take me, via two lovely village churches, up the Lee Valley to the next important medieval pilgrim centre: the town of Ware.

St James with his pilgrim staff, depicted on the font at St Mary's church in Ware

PRACTICAL INFORMATION

Route overview   13.2 miles (21.2km)

The start and end points of this stage are easily accessible by train, as is Broxbourne, a point at which the stage can easily be divided. As the railway shadows the route throughout, there are several other spots at which you can leave or re-join the path.

From Waltham Abbey it is **1.3 miles** by road to Waltham Cross, then **0.4 miles** to the open country of the River Lee Country Park. After just over another **1 mile** you reach the River Lee Navigation, and follow its towpath for **3.3 miles** to the outskirts of Broxbourne. The route is almost completely flat until you leave the river and walk via Broxbourne Old Mill for a short uphill segment to Broxbourne Park, and St Augustine's, reached in a further **0.2 miles**. Broxbourne railway station, where the stage can be easily divided, is another **0.2 miles**.

From Broxbourne railway station the route follows the New River Path, also the Hertfordshire Way, which are both signposted, to Rye House **(2 miles)**. Here you switch to the River Lee Navigation for **3.1 miles**, then bear west for a short climb to St John the Baptist in Great Amwell, reached in **0.3 miles**. From here it is **2 miles**, first on the New River, then the River Lee Navigation (re-joining the Hertfordshire Way), to the end of this stage at St Mary's, Ware.

Public transport options

This entire stage is easily accessible by **train**, with stations at Waltham Cross (1 mile from Waltham Abbey), Cheshunt, Broxbourne, Rye House, Stanstead St Margarets and Ware (half a mile from the end of the stage). The No 310 **bus** service connects the start and end with most points along the way, and Central Connect's No 351 stops in St Margarets, Great Amwell and Ware. See also public transport map and table pp29-31.

Where to eat or stay along the way

● **Waltham Abbey** (see Stage 1, pp35-6)
● **Cheshunt** (after 3 miles/4.8km) Budget **accommodation** is available at *Lea Valley Youth Hostel* (🖳 yha.org.uk), 100yds off the route.
● **Broxbourne** (after 6 miles/9.6km) Single, twin and double **rooms** are available at *Kingsway Bed and Breakfast* (☎ 07539-219947, 🖳 bedandbreakfastbroxbourne.co.uk; 19 High Rd; shared bathrooms) half a mile from route. **Food** is available at the *Crown* (☎

● **Terrain** Mostly flat, mainly well-maintained towpaths
● **Difficulty** Easy
● **Cumulative distance from London** 30.9 miles (49.7km)
● **Time** 4hrs 30mins actual walking time
● **Total ascent** 141m, 462ft
● **Map** OS Explorer *174 Epping Forest & Lee Valley*
● **GPX route file & directions*** 502.pdf, 502.gpx, 502.kml at 🖳 https://trailblazer-guides.com/press * See pp27-8 for more information on downloads

01992-462244; daily noon-9pm; Old Nazeing Rd), an airy riverside pub with garden.

● **Rye Station** (after 8.6 miles/13.8km) For real ales and **pub grub** in a 19th-century inn with riverside garden head to *The Rye House* (☎ 01992-465151, 🖳 greeneking-pubs.co.uk /pubs/hertfordshire/rye-house, Rye Rd; daily 11am-11pm, food noon-9pm).

● **Stanstead St Margarets** (after 10 miles/ 16.2km) Offering **food**, real ales and a riverside garden is the *Jolly Fisherman* (☎ 01920-870125, 🖳 mcmullens.co.uk/jollyfisherman, 8 Station Rd; open Mon-Thur noon-11pm, Fri & Sat noon-midnight, Sun noon-10.30pm, food Mon-Sat noon-9pm, Sun noon-8pm).

● **Gt Amwell** (after 11.1 miles/17.9km) Country pub *George IV* (☎ 01920-870039, 🖳 georgeivpub.co.uk, Cautherly Lane; Tue-Fri noon-3.30pm, 5pm-11pm, Sat noon-11pm, Sun noon-6pm, Mon closed; food hours check with pub) has an excellent **restaurant**.

● **Ware** There are several **accommodation** options including: *The Tap Bar Bed and Breakfast* (☎ 01920-468549, 🖳 brewerytap-ware.co.uk, 83 High St; 4 en-suite rooms) which also does **food** (see below); *Café Frappe & Bed and Breakfast* (☎ 01920-469766; 2 New Rd) and *Premier Inn* (☎ 03330-033405, 🖳 premierinn.com; Marsh Lane) within 500yds of route. For **breakfast** or **lunch**, seek out *Ware Café* (Mon-Sat 6.30am-4pm, Sun closed; 43 West St) serving breakfasts, hot meals, sandwiches. *Bridget's Tearoom* at Ware Priory (🖳 facebook.com, search Bridgets ASL; Mon-Sat 10.30am-3.30pm; Fletcher's Lea, High St) and *Milady Tea and Coffee Lounge* (☎ 01920-469997; Mon & Wed-Sun 9am-4pm; 12 High St) are both popular for **afternoon teas**. If it's an **evening meal** you're looking for try *The Tap Bar* (see above; open daily noon-10pm, food noon-3pm), a traditional pie, ale and cider house.

Services

● **Waltham Abbey** (see Stage 1, pp35-6)
● **Ware** For **groceries** there's Tesco (5-6 West St; Mon-Sat 6am-midnight; Sun 11am-5pm) or Costcutter (20 Amwell End; daily 7am-11pm)

2

PILGRIMAGE HIGHLIGHTS

- **Waltham Abbey** *Church of Holy Cross and St Lawrence* (☎ 01992-767897, ⌨ walthamabbeychurch.co.uk, 4 Church St; open Mon, Tue, Thur, Fri, Sat 10am-4pm, Wed 11am-4pm, Sun noon-4pm, services, see website for current times). **Pilgrim stamp in church.** *Waltham Abbey Gatehouse, Bridge and gardens* (⌨ english-heritage.org.uk, Abbey View; open during daylight hours;)
- **Waltham Cross** *Eleanor Cross* on route at junction of Eleanor Cross Rd / High St.
- **Broxbourne** *St Augustine's* (☎ 01992-444117, ⌨ staugustinesbroxbourne.org.uk, Churchfields; open Mon-Wed & Fri 9.30am-1pm, services Sun 8am except 1st in month, 9.30am, 11am, 6pm)
- **Great Amwell** *St John the Baptist* (☎ 01920-870115, ⌨ achurchnearyou.com/church/7880, St John's Lane; for opening contact keyholders listed on notice board; services 1st & 3rd Sun 9am). **Pilgrim stamp in church.**

For details on pilgrim points in Ware, see Stage 3, p62

Waltham Abbey

The Church of the Holy Cross and St Lawrence carries a big name and a remarkable history, but has a rather diminished, apologetic appearance as it peeks at me from the end of Highbridge St. As well it might. Rather like an ecclesiastical version of the Black Knight in *Monty Python and the Holy Grail*, a one-time abbey church that was among the largest and finest in England has had great lumps hacked off it.

What survives is a mere stump, part of the nave – or torso if you like – from which the head and legs are missing. What hasn't been amputated from Waltham's abbey church has been patched and mended. Yellow and orange brick mix with cream stone to make the walls a patchwork. It takes a sustained effort of imagination to picture this as part of one of the greatest monasteries in the country, but enough is left that, the more I explore, the more I come to appreciate what a place this was.

Just to the north of the church's west door flows Cornmill Stream. I trace it, past a weir against which a duck ladder is care-

fully placed, to the surviving abbey gatehouse. Here it was that monks, pilgrims and kings left the boats that had ferried them up the Lea from London to enter this great Augustinian abbey.

I follow in their footsteps, walking past the surviving passageway that led into the cloister, now just a ghost sketched out in the grass, and round to the east end of the church. Here I come upon what must, historically, be one of the most significant patches of ground in all England. A simple memorial slab and square stump of stone

Above: Waltham Abbey and the River Lea.
Right: King Harold was buried here in 1066; a simple stone memorial marks the spot.

HAROLD
KING OF
ENGLAND
OBIT 1066

A HOLY CROSS AND KING HAROLD

King Harold

Pilgrims came to Waltham Abbey from the 11th to the 16th centuries because of a miracle-working holy cross to which was attached a powerful story.

The legend is that, some years before the Norman Conquest, a Somerset nobleman called Tofig or Toley had a vision, in which he was told that if he dug on St Michael's Hill in Montacute, Somerset, he would find a holy cross. He did so, and unearthed a Purbeck marble crucifix which was christened the Montacute Cross. He brought it to Waltham, where he also had land, and placed it in the church.

The cross quickly drew pilgrims seeking cures. Among them was Harold Godwinson, Earl of Essex and East Anglia, the future King Harold, who was suffering from paralysis. Harold was cured and, in 1060, he rebuilt the church in gratitude, dedicating it to the Holy Cross. Edward the Confessor, Harold's predecessor as king, attended the ceremony. To give a little Walsingham Camino perspective: the apparition of Our Lady of Walsingham appeared to Richeldis the following year, and she set about building the Holy House. When Harold was killed at the Battle of Hastings, in 1066, his body was brought here and buried under the high altar.

In 1177 Henry II comes into the story. As part of his penance following the murder of Archbishop Thomas Becket, he undertook a massive building project, trebling the size of the church, and established this as an Augustinian abbey.

Henry VIII was particularly fond of Waltham, coming here regularly, up the river alongside which I walked yesterday, to escape the pressures of London, to hunt and to converse with the abbot. At the time of the Dissolution, the abbey had great status, and its church very nearly became a cathedral. Instead, it was reduced to a stub, and the Holy Cross was lost.

mark the point where the tomb of King Harold, defeated and slain at the battle of Hastings, once lay beneath the high altar.

I enter the church. I'm not expecting much but, once inside, things are a lot more uplifting. The Victorians performed some very sympathetic cosmetic surgery here. From the bare bones left after centuries of abuse and neglect, they created a church that looks and feels wholly Norman. The nave, an echo of that at Durham with its great fluted columns, acquired a brightly coloured diamond-patterned roof bearing the signs of the zodiac, modelled on that at Peterborough. The reredos shows the nativity, with a frieze of Aesop's fables. Shining above them, like a great stained-glass sun, is a rose window by Burne Jones. In the Lady Chapel, there is the genuinely medieval wall painting of The Last Judgement.

Left: Waltham Abbey, interior. **Right**: Revealed when the whitewash covering it was removed in 1876, the mural of the Last Judgement dates from the early 15th century.(Photos Poliphilo, CC0 1.0)

Back in the churchyard, I duck out south through the archway beneath the Welsh Harp pub into Market Square, from which 13th century Sun St runs east. Pre-Reformation, pilgrimage sustained this town, and as I wander around I see there are still several inns with medieval roots. There has probably been an inn on the site of the *Welsh Harp* for at least 600 years, and on that of the Green Dragon for almost as long.

Waltham Abbey to Waltham Cross

There is a rare start on tarmac on the first stage of today's walk from Waltham Abbey. It's a mundane stretch of road ending in a hallucination. Or what feels like one. Walking down a nondescript pedestrianised street I'm unprepared for the remarkable sight of a 70ft spire of ornately carved stonework rising like a gothic rocket from the dirty, chewing-gum flecked paving of the town's central crossroads. But there – flanked by a vape

Eleanor Cross

store, a phone shop, a bank and a takeaway – it is: the Eleanor Cross. But what is it, and why is it here?

In 1290, when Edward I's wife Eleanor of Castille died at Harby, near Lincoln, her funeral cortege took a winding route to Westminster Abbey, where she was to be buried. The king had commemorative crosses erected at each of the 12 places her body rested overnight, one being at today's starting point, Waltham Abbey. It was placed here, on Ermine Street, because the abbey already had the Montacute Cross, and didn't see the need for another. But placing it right on Ermine Street meant it would be seen by many more travellers. Medieval pilgrims on their way to Walsingham would pause at the Eleanor Cross, and I do too.

Immediately north and south of the cross were two coaching inns – both gone – the Four Swans and the Falcon. The Falcon was built, in

2

1617, actually abutting the cross. In 1891, when the Falcon was demolished, it was found to contain the remains of a chantry chapel, where Masses were offered for the repose of the soul of Queen Eleanor.

From the Eleanor Cross I walk up Ermine Street, now the pedestrianised High St, and follow the old pilgrim route until I reach Trinity Lane, then turn east for the River Lee Country Park, and regain my path upriver.

Above: River Lee Country Park

River Lee Country Park

This is a place of regeneration. A landscape pitted with sand and gravel pits has been transformed into a 1,000-acre nature reserve, the flooded pits forming a string of great lakes. I come across an intriguing sculpture by the path, called The Shrine. A sign says it features 'nature's watcher, the Green Man'. A great leaf-fringed head, carved from a giant cedar, towers above the path, flanked by two benches, their high backs carved with oak leaves.

At Waltham Common Lock, the lakes close in. Barely a sliver of land divides the River Lee Navigation from the lakes on either side, yet somehow the canal manages to keep its waters to itself as it runs north between Cheshunt Lake, Turnershill Marsh and Hollyfield Lake.

The air is briny and fresh. Nothing

Above: Greylag goose, River Lee Country Park

soaks up stress like walking alongside still waters such as these. As I tramp on I sense I am slipping deeper into the state of calm and contemplation that pilgrimage brings.

Nature is drawing me in, and what nature it is. The Lee Valley's rich mix of wetland, water meadow, reed bed, woodland, hedges and field margins provide a habitat for a wide range of birds. Bittern and smew winter in the reedbeds; whitethroat and yellowhammer are at home in the hedges; kestrel and barn owl favour the long grass of the meadows; lapwing the cultivated fields; nightingale the woods. There are watervole and otter.

In winter, the lakes are home to huge numbers of gadwall and shoveler ducks, and waders such as snipe.

Today, my own bird spotting is more modest. I spy a cormorant on the far bank. Two greylag geese slip into the flow and glide along, dipping their beaks into the water to savour it with a 'tup tup tup' as if at a wine tasting. A family of swans fly overhead on squeaky wings.

There is a human river community too: so many boats moored, from old but much-loved narrowboats to modern steel barges and a mix of cruisers, some spanking new, others aged and quietly sinking. I'm particularly taken by the recycled oil rig lifeboats, bulbous orange things linked up like a string of saveloys.

The park continues all the way to Broxbourne, and because I simply follow the towpath all the way, I have no need even to glance at a map. The locks tick off the miles, each with a lockkeeper's cottage, hinting at an idyllic life to be enjoyed there.

Above: A wide variety of houseboats line the banks of the Lee

Broxbourne

At Broxbourne I reach the half-way mark of this stage. With the *Crown* by the path just before the village, and two more pubs close to St Augustine's church, this makes an ideal spot for lunch. Just after passing the Crown I swap waterways. Leaving the Navigation, I loop east to meet the River Lee and follow it beneath the railway and over a meadow to Broxbourne Old Mill. It's a quiet, grassy spot, ideal for a picnic.

There was a mill here for 900 years, until it burned down in 1949. The waters foam through a pit containing the remains of its mechanism, surrounded by the stump of stone walls. The mill was part of the manor of Broxbourne, held from 1544 until the Reformation by the Knights of St John of Jerusalem, also known as the Knights Templar, who guided pilgrims to Jerusalem.

I cross the river and swing north to climb Mill Lane. On the rise above me, the crenellated flint tower of St Augustine's peaks above the treetops. I come out before the church at the foot of Broxbourne Park, an avenue of trees running from its door across the expanse of grass.

It's the sort of landscape you want to step into, and if I

Broxbourne Church

did I would quickly reach ancient Ermine Street, which runs just beyond the park. Yet another river – New River – runs past the church door, and I shall follow it north to Rye House. I sit beside it to eat my lunch before, replenished, I enter the church. It's dark and atmospheric with its sombre wooden ceiling, pillared arches and abundance of monuments and effigies. In the south aisle, is a memorial to John Loudon McAdam, who invented the process of tarmacking roads: hence 'tarmacadam'.

Broxbourne to Rye House

Turning right out of the churchyard I walk, with renewed appreciation, on Mr McAdam's very handy invention, and pass Broxbourne railway station, where a sign for New River Path points me on my way. Actually, the New River is neither new, nor a river. It is in fact a water supply viaduct, completed in 1613, to bring drinking water from Hertfordshire to quench the thirst of London. Water to feed it is drawn from streams, springs and boreholes deep beneath the river itself, to supply 48 million gallons a day, 8 per cent of London's needs.

The landscape is a good deal more suburban after Broxbourne. Back gardens line the New River, in contrast to the reed beds along the Lea, and the houses crowd in ever tighter as I approach Rye House.

Rye House to Great Amwell

On a modern map, Rye House is the name of a railway station and a pub, but the original Rye House was a moated medieval manor house. Only the gatehouse survives, beside my path. This is a place with a close connection to the man who casts a shadow over my pilgrim path: Henry VIII. For this was the childhood home of Katherine Parr, later to become his sixth wife.

From the river, the gatehouse is just a blank brick wall with a spindly, barley-sugar chimney twizzling up from it. You need to walk around to the far side to appreciate something of the manor's grandeur. Here, the rest of the house is mapped out in brick lines laid in the grass.

As I walk on towards Great Amwell, things become increasingly rural once more, the river threading again through flooded gravel pits and nature reserves.

Great Amwell to Ware

Like Broxbourne, Great Amwell sits perched on the very edge of the high ground to the west of the Lee Valley. I glimpse 11th century St John the Baptist high above me, its tower topped with a slim slate spire, in a thicket of ancient yews. I climb a narrow dark path that barely squeezes through the trees, finally pounding a set of steep steps to reach the bottom corner of the churchyard. This is a magical, sequestered spot: like a childhood hide-out.

I pass a rather bare, yellow brick neo-Classical mausoleum beside the path as I enter the churchyard. If it weren't for the ornate fluted urn perched on a pedestal on the roof I might have taken it for an outhouse. In fact, this is the mausoleum of the Mylne family, built by Robert Mylne to commemorate the deaths of his wife,

---

RYE HOUSE – THE CHILDHOOD HOME OF HENRY'S SIXTH WIFE

Rye House was the main family home for the Parrs from 1517, and Katherine and her sister Anne remained here after their father's death, when she was only five, until 1531. She married the king in 1543 and outlived him.

Katherine's links to Henry began in childhood. At the age of 12, her brother William was sent away to be brought up in the household of Henry VIII's illegitimate son Henry FitzRoy, who I shall encounter when I reach Thetford. Henry was Katherine's third husband, and she would go on to have another. She was multi-lingual, strongly Protestant and, in the year of her marriage to Henry, published anonymously a book called *Psalms or Prayers*. Katherine later published two more religious books under her own name – *Prayers or Meditations* and *The Lamentation of a Sinner*.

Above: The gatehouse is all that is left of Rye House. **Below**: Amwell Pool and the memorial stone.

Maria, two daughters and a son in the same year, 1790.

Mylne, an engineer, is buried not here but in St Paul's Cathedral, where he was surveyor of the fabric, close to Sir Christopher Wren. He was also, most pertinent to my walk, the engineer of the New River aqueduct, and hence responsible for the waterway I have been following.

An avenue of yews lines the main path to the church's north door, the dark oak panels peeking invitingly through the greenery. St John the Baptist is a perfect place for pilgrim reflection (Norman apart from the tower) and I slip inside.

From the church I drop down again to the New River, reaching it at Amwell Pool, where the waters divide around two neat oval islands, carefully walled off from the water. On the one closest to me is a stone memorial, created by Robert Mylne to honour Sir Hugh Myddelton, mastermind of the New River project. It reads:

Perpetual be thy stream,
Nor e'er thy springs be less
Which thousands drink who never dream

Whence flows the boon they bless.
Too often thus ungrateful man
Blind and unconscious lives,
Enjoys kind Heaven's indulgent plan,
Nor thinks of Him who gives.

These lines give me something to ponder as I move on, swapping from New River to Navigation for the final approach to Ware, where I shall walk Ermine Street for a stretch. As I walk, I reflect that medieval pilgrims would have understood exactly that water is a sacred gift, and would have attributed healing powers to it. This pilgrimage is giving me an opportunity to step out of my 'blind and unconscious' life and to 'think of Him who gives.'

3

Ware to Stansted Mountfitchet

From the pilgrim town of Ware to Bishop's Stortford via the River Ash valley, then on alongside the River Stort to Stansted Mountfitchet

Many a weary pilgrim has found rest in Ware. What is now the High St was known in medieval times as Walsingham Way, and the many former inns

that housed those pilgrims can still be identified from the archways leading to their stable yards. Like medieval pilgrims, I stop off at the church of St Mary, and Ware Priory, before setting off across the rolling hills of Hertfordshire. Along the way, three very traditional English churches with soaring Hertfordshire Spike spires, and a pair of delightfully unexpected Italian Romanesque and Renaissance-inspired gems, line the way to Bishop's Stortford. From there, a riverside ramble beside the Stort delivers me to today's destination: Stansted Mountfitchet.

Just off the route at Perry Green, near Much Hadham, is the **Henry Moore Sculpture Park** with works including *Large Reclining Figure*

PRACTICAL INFORMATION

Route overview   16.4 miles (26.4km)

Largely following the Hertfordshire Way. The start and end of this stage are both easily accessible by train, as is Bishop's Stortford, about three quarters of the way in, and all have accommodation options. The approximate halfway point, Much Hadham, offers refreshment but not accommodation, although it does have a regular bus service to and from Bishop's Stortford.

Today's walk from Ware is over generally gentle, easy-going country. An initial section takes you up the Ash valley, reaching the village of Wareside, with its church and two pubs, in **3.7 miles**; then climbing gently to Widford's church in a further **1.6 miles**. From here a plunge back into the Ash valley takes you to Much Hadham, with pub and shared Anglican/Catholic church, for lunch after another **3.3 miles**.

Then comes the only climb of the walk, a short scramble up to ride the tops to Bishop's Stortford, with two churches and many pubs and cafés, in **4.5 miles**. A final stretch along the River Stort brings you to Stansted Mountfitchet in **3.3 miles**.

Public transport options

The start and end points of this stage are connected by **train**, with stations at Ware, Bishop's Stortford and Stansted Mountfitchet. Central Connect's No 351 **bus** calls at Widford, the halfway point at Much Hadham (outside Ye Olde Red Lion, now a private house) and Bishop's Stortford, and the No 301 runs between Bishop's Stortford and Stansted Mountfitchet. See also public transport map and table pp29-31.

If you need a **taxi**, Much Hadham-based *Tracey's Travel* (☎ 01279-843344, 💻 traceys-travel.business.site; 105 Windmill Way) is among firms serving the area.

Where to eat or stay along the way

● **Ware** (see Stage 2, p49)
● **Wareside** (after 4 miles/6.5km) Stop for **refreshments** at *The Chequers* (☎ 01920-467010, 💻 chequerswareside.com; food Mon-Sat noon-2pm & 6-8.30pm, Sun noon-2.45pm & 6-8pm) or *The White Horse* (☎ 01920-464433, 💻 whitehorsefh.co.uk; Tue-Sun noon-late, Mon closed), two adjacent, very pleasant country inns.
● **Much Hadham** (after 8.3 miles/13.4km) *The Bull Inn* (☎ 01279-841100, 💻 the bullmh.co.uk, High St; Tue-Sat noon-10pm, food to 8pm, Sun noon-8pm, food to 5pm, Mon closed) is a charming village inn with good **pub grub**.

● **Terrain** Rolling countryside   ● **Difficulty** Moderate
● **Cumulative distance from London** 47.3 miles (76.1km)
● **Time** 5hrs 50mins actual walking time   ● **Total ascent** 337m/1105ft
● **Map** OS Explorer 194 *Hertford & Bishop's Stortford; 195 Braintree & Saffron Walden*
● **GPX route file & directions*** 503.pdf,503.gpx, 503.kml at 💻 https://trailblazer-guides.com/press * See pp27-8 for more information on downloads

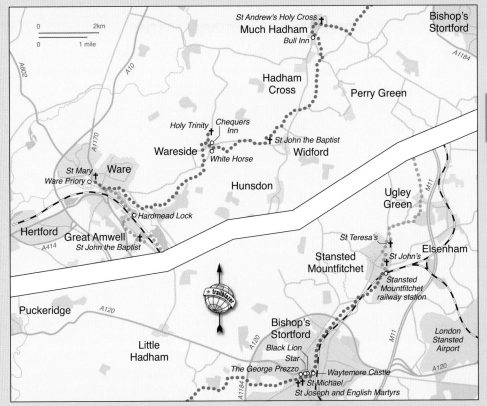

● **Bishop's Stortford** (after 13.3miles/21.4km) has options to **stay**, including the family-run *Jolly Brewers* (☎ 01279-836055, 🖳 stansted-hotels-jollybrewers.com) at 70 South St. For a **meal**, choices include: family pizza restaurant *The George, Prezzo* (☎ 01279-656784, 🖳 prezzorestaurants.co.uk, North St; Mon-Thur noon-10pm, Fri-Sun 11.30am-10.30pm); 16th century inn *Black Lion* (☎ 01279-654232, 🖳 facebook.com/theblacklion publichouse, 10 Bridge St; open daily 4pm-late); and 17th century inn *The Star* (☎ 01279 654211, 🖳 craft-pubs.co.uk/thestar-bishopsstortford; food Mon-Fri 11am-10pm, Sat & Sun noon-10pm; 7 Bridge St) with real ales and pub grub.

● **Stansted Mountfitchet Stay** and **eat** at *The Kings Arms Hotel*, (☎ 01279-248170, 🖳 ourlocal.pub/pubs/kings-arms-hotel-stansted, Station Rd; open daily 10am-11pm, food to 8.30pm), a characterful village pub with 4 en-suite rooms. Breakfast, lunch, snacks, at *Café Yeomans* (☎ 01279-817755, 14 Lower St; Mon-Sat 8am-4pm, Sun 9am-2.30pm).

Services
● **Ware** (see Stage 2, p49)
● **Bishop's Stortford** For **supermarket** supplies there's Sainsbury's (Mon-Sat 7.30am-10pm, Sun 10am-4pm; 16 Jackson Sq) and Tesco (daily 6am-11pm; 32a South St). For **laundry**: Suds (☎ 01279-866183; Mon-Fri 9am-4pm, Sat/Sun 9am-6pm; 12 London Rd).
● **Stansted Mountfitchet** has a Co-op (daily 7am-10pm) on Church Rd.

PILGRIMAGE HIGHLIGHTS

- **Ware** *St Mary's* (☎ 01920-319236, 🖥 achurchnearyou.com/church/7901, Church St; open daily 9am-5.30pm, services Mon-Thur 9.15am & 5pm, Sun 8am & 10am;). **Pilgrim stamp in church.** *Ware Priory*, (grounds open 8am-8pm or dusk if earlier; High St) is now a wedding and functions venue.
- **Wareside** Don't miss glorious Romanesque gem *Holy Trinity* (☎ 01920-877276, 🖥 hwwchurch.org.uk/wareside-holy-trinity; open for services 2nd&4th Sun 9.30am).
- **Widford** Lovely country church *St John the Baptist* (☎ 01920-877276, 🖥 achurchnearyou.com/church/7904, Ware Rd; services 1st & 3rd Sun 9.30am) has a holy cross beside the churchyard.
- **Much Hadham** At *St Andrew's Holy Cross* both Anglican and Catholic communions meet. *St Andrews* (☎ 01279 842609, 🖥 riverashchurches.org.uk, Church Lane; open for services, Sun 9.15). *Holy Cross* (☎ 01279-654063, 🖥 rcstortford.org.uk; open for services Sun 11.30am) Adorned with works by the sculptor Henry Moore. **Pilgrim stamp in church.**
- **Bishop's Stortford** *St Michael's* (☎ 01279-654416, 🖥 saintmichaelweb.org.uk, Windhill; open 'early morning to mid afternoon', services Sun 8am & 10am) is an Anglican parish church. Catholic *St Joseph and the English Martyrs* (☎ 01279-654063, 🖥 rcstortford.org.uk, 3 Windhill; open for services Mon-Fri 9.30am, Sat 6pm, Sun 9am & 11am) is modelled on a Florentine Renaissance church.

For Stansted Mountfitchet pilgrimage highlights, see Stage 4 p76.

The pilgrim town of Ware

It is the simplest of gestures to make. I raise my hand, reach out, and touch the figure of St James (see p46) carrying his pilgrim staff and leather water bottle, carved into the 14th century font in the church of St Mary the Virgin. But, in doing so, I reach across the centuries. Back to the time, pre-Reformation, when medieval pilgrims entered this church, saw this font, and perhaps touched this very same figure.

St Christopher

St Mary's started life as the chapel of Ware Priory, and today's flint church, its 14th-century tower topped by a stiletto-sharp spire known as a Hertfordshire Spike, has been much altered over the centuries. Nevertheless, I find a spark of solace in the fact that, with all that has been fractured and lost from the tradition of pilgrimage in England, such a symbol should survive as a link between the pilgrims of old and me, today.

I make a circuit of the font before I set out on today's walk, and find also St Christo-

Above left: A blue plaque marks the location of the original Ware Priory.
Above right: Ware Priory today, originally Ware Friary.

pher, patron saint of travellers, bearing the young Christ on his shoulder, among the other saints and angels. I petition a blessing from St Christopher and St James before stepping out into a spring day that holds the promise of sun and blue skies.

Ware Priory was probably beside the church, the site bounded today by Church St to the north, and West St to the south. But, confusingly, the handsome, white-rendered building I can see across the High St from St Mary's, and which is now called Ware Priory, is *not* that institution. It is actually on the site of a later Franciscan friary, of which more in a moment.

First, I walk along Church St to No. 9, and a trace of the original priory. Here a blue plaque reads: 'The Manor House, formerly known as the Rectory Manor. Once part of the Benedictine Priory of Ware.' This house may have stood at the southeastern corner of the cloister. There is a theory that the upper floor, with its heavy medieval beams, was the monks' dormitory, but Historic England now considers this unlikely.

I walk back past St Mary's, to what is now called Ware Priory, but was actually Ware Friary. The friary occupied a seven-acre site on the north bank of the River Lee, and consisted of a chapel, cloister, a great hall, and accommodation for friars and guests. It was seized by the Crown at the Reformation and became a private house.

In 1919 it was given to the people of Ware. The surviving buildings, some of which date from the 14th century, are a venue for weddings and other events, with the present Priory Hall in what was the cloister; the open archways glazed to create a room. The glorious seven-acre riverside grounds are a public park, complete with an open-air swimming pool, the Lido. I'm tempted to linger here, but these boots were made for walking...

Leaving Ware

I shoulder my pack, point my face into the sun, and walk east down the High St. Ware did very good trade as a pilgrim town. Chaucer mentions it in *The Canterbury Tales*, as the town where the Cook lived, and the stretch of Ermine Street I am walking along was known as Walsingham Way.

This road was lined with numerous inns, and the many arched entrances to what were once their stable yards survive within properties that have long since found another use.

Above: The path follows the valley of the River Ash

Star St takes me quickly to the edge of town, where a 'Public Footpath' fingerpost leads me down an earth track, past allotments where tentative, early-morning gardeners are discussing whether they should put their potatoes in. It's April, but a cold snap is forecast.

The track takes me out to meadows that fall gently down to the watery valley of the Lee, where the God-given river and the man-made Navigation flow either side of a long, still lake, all three fringed with willows and reed-beds. While the slope tugs me right, the path pulls me left, and I climb to reach a gap in the hedge, where I vault a stile and cross Hollywell Rd, to reach a serpentine track that drops me down into the valley of the River Ash.

Along the River Ash to Wareside

A footbridge carries me over the Ash to the track of an old railway, which once ran north to Much Hadham and beyond. I'll walk along its path for stretches, but mainly I'll be following the Hertfordshire Way. On this subterranean stretch the rabbits have taken up residence, a great warren pockmarking the banks of the cutting.

I leave the enclosure of the old, hedge-fringed rail line for a stretch across glorious parkland, dotted with oak, elm and pine, the grass nibbled lawn-perfect. The Ash is a modest river compared with the Lee and its siblings, which I followed on the two previous stages of this pilgrimage, but it's a faithful companion as I head north; here tumbling over a weir to my left.

On the rise ahead of me, and marked on my map as The Dairy Farm, is a clutch of elegant red-brick Victorian Gothic buildings designed by Alfred Waterhouse, best known for the Natural History Museum in London. These are part of the Easneye Estate, and Waterhouse also built Easneye

Above: Easneye Chapel. The Easneye Estate, designed by Alfred Waterhouse, architect of London's Natural History Museum. **Below**: The Dairy Farm.

Mansion, hidden in the woods at the top of the rise, for Sir Thomas Buxton, of a Quaker brewing family, in 1868. The main dairy building has a great tower above a central archway, topped with a dovecot beneath a pitched roof. It bears a terracotta shield on which the Buxton motto reads: 'Do it with thy might'. Alongside it is a little octagonal chapel.

After a woodland stretch I pick up the old railway line again, to Mardocks Mill, then follow a concrete farm track that climbs towards the village of Wareside, a sequestered place where cottages cluster around a wish-bone of lanes hunkered along the banks of another, much smaller river, the Nimney Bourne.

I am in the heart of the country, finally well away from London and its environs, and I feel my pilgrim journey is truly underway. I can slip into sustained periods of solitude and reflection.

Above: Romanesque Holy Trinity, Wareside.

Wareside to Widford

Holy Trinity, Wareside is a very exotic addition to this very English village. It is modelled on 12th century Italian Romanesque, in mellow yellow brick, with an elegant octagonal bell turret clutched in the angle between nave and north transept and a Romanesque wheel window above the west gable entrance. The church stands in a graveyard shaggy with grass and speckled with daffodils.

The church is not the only pilgrim treasure in Wareside. It also has two pubs: the *White Horse* and the *Chequers Inn*, both on the B1004 as the Hertfordshire Way leaves the village. Just beyond the latter, this long-distance path takes me back to the River Ash, alongside which I walk to regain the old railway track, and approach the next village, Widford, and another lovely church. The oldest parts of St John the Baptist, Widford, are 13th century, but the fragments of an earlier church contained in its walls, and the Saxon bones found nearby, suggest a much older place of worship. Like St Mary's in Ware, its stolid, earth-bound flint tower is topped by a contrasting slim, sharp spike that pierces the heavens.

Above: St John the Baptist, Widford (**left**) and the view from the churchyard (**right**).

Beside the churchyard is a little paved courtyard, enclosed by an ancient red-brick wall with, at its centre, a holy cross. The inscription on it reads: 'We adore thee oh Christ and we bless thee because by thy holy cross thou hast redeemed the world'.

Widford to Much Hadham

The Hertfordshire Way runs right through the churchyard of St John the Baptist, to reveal a stunning vista. I am on the lip of the Ash valley, gazing way over to Crackney Wood. Below me is spread a lush green descent; a wide path of flattened grass drawing me onward. A bench in

Our Lady of Walsingham (**above**) in St Andrew's Holy Cross, Much Hadham (**below**)

the churchyard allows me to savour the view, and give thanks, before stepping down into it.

On the valley floor I am once again tracking the River Ash upstream, deep into the countryside: a place of scattered farms and occasional grand houses; of woodland now carpeted with pale yellow primroses. Soon, bluebells will replace them, and form a low-lying mist of dusty blue through Mill Wood and Sidehill Wood.

When I reach Much Hadham, I've walked eight miles, half my total, and it's time for a break. I walk to the church up the long village High St,

Above: The Tree of Life Window (**left**) at St Andrew's Holy Cross, Much Hadham, based on an etching by Henry Moore, and an admonition above the door (**right**).

where the rendered walls of the many timber-framed medieval houses are painted in an array of sugar Easter-egg shades: pale pink, powder blue, duck egg, primrose and white.

I have timed my arrival for Mass. I get a very friendly pilgrim welcome at the church. The priest, Fr Antonio, comes to chat before Mass and, after it, a parishioner proudly fills me in on church history.

ST ANDREW AND HOLY CROSS, MUCH HADHAM

This church's twin dedications reflect the fact that it is shared by Anglicans (the St Andrew part) and Catholic (Holy Cross), making it a model of practical ecumenism, and one that might be beneficially replicated in many other country churches snaffled after the Reformation.

Much Hadham has a long royal and ecclesiastical history. Tucked behind the churchyard is the Bishop's Palace, the summer retreat of the Bishops of London from before the Norman Conquest until 1647. It is now divided into three private houses.

The fact that the Bishops of London holidayed next door accounts for the size and grandeur of this glorious, 13th-century flint church, its tower again surmounted by a Hertfordshire spike. The bishop's door survives in the north wall.

The sculptor Henry Moore, who lived a couple of miles away in Perry Green, carved the two elegant heads of a king and queen (**right**) placed on either side of the west door. The window above that door includes a Tree of Life based on an etching by him. Between door and window is the inscription: 'And this is the Gate of Heaven.'

There is a little statue of Our Lady of Walsingham on the south side of the sanctuary, alongside a rather lovely bronze of Mary Magdalen. There are kneelers dedicated to each of the apostles including, unusually, Judas. His bears the symbol of a rope.

Another rarity is the Easter Sepulchre, most of which were destroyed at the Reformation. In the Middle Ages it was the custom to move the Blessed Sacrament from the high altar on Good Friday and place it in this Easter tomb. It would be returned to the high altar on Easter Sunday for the celebration of the Resurrection, hence symbolising the journey from death to risen life.

I am waved on my way as I leave through the south porch, walking beneath an oak ceiling featuring an angel choir, and the admonition above the outer door: 'Go and sin no more'. I'll do my best. Walking should keep me on the straight and narrow.

Much Hadham to Bishop's Stortford
After a hearty pilgrim lunch in the cosy, stone-flagged bar of *The Bull*, I continue on my way, following the Herts Way down a narrow tree-shaded path beside the

churchyard and on to the only real climb on this stage: the scramble up through the woods to emerge on the heights of Winding Hill. Here the short, overwintered stubble left after last year's harvest drapes the landscape in suede (**above**).

Below: Bishop's Stortford St Michael's

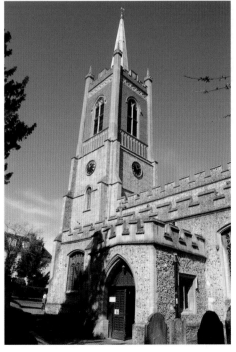

3

THE TWO CHURCHES OF BISHOPS STORTFORD

Italian Renaissance-style St Joseph and the English Martyrs, with its gold star-studded ceiling and elaborate Carrara marble high altar surmounted by a grand four-poster *baldacchino*, or canopy, was inspired by the Florentine church of San Miniato al Monte.

A few doors down is the very traditional, Anglican, St Michael's. There was probably a timber church on this site from the 7th century, but the Normans built anew in the early 12th. The vault survives, as does a Purbeck marble font from 1150.

After the Reformation the rood loft, which supported the figures of Christ on the Cross, St Mary and St John, was hacked down and sold off. A beam from it is said to form the mantlepiece above the fireplace in the bar of the 15th century former Boar's Head Inn, now a Turkish restaurant, across the road from the church.

Above: Window in St Michael's

I continue on this relatively high country to Bishop's Stortford, at the outskirts of which I cross the grounds of Hillmead Primary School and Bishop Stortford College on my way to the town centre, and two more wonderful churches.

Windhill drops gently to the town-centre crossroads, passing Catholic St Joseph and the English Martyrs church, and its near neighbour, Anglican St Michael's church. A narrow way called Palmers Lane may reference the pilgrims who passed

Above: The 16th century Black Lion, Bishops Stortford

through this town, the word referring to the devout, who carried a palm on their journey to Walsingham and other shrines.

Bishop's Stortford to Stansted Mountfitchet

Leaving Bishop's Stortford I pass the earth mound of Waytemore Castle, built as a motte and bailey defence by the Normans, then enter the first of a series of carefully managed landscapes that take me almost all the way to Stansted Mountfitchet. I am in the Stort Valley, walking through what was once a marshy floodplain, colonised by willows and black poplars, but is now dry, the River Stort well-marshalled.

I pass through Grange Paddocks Meadow, used for summer grazing; and into Bat Willow Hurst, where reedbeds fill the area between river and railway. 'Bat Willow' refers to the fact that the damp marshy ground was ideal for the cricket bat willow tree (*Salix alba var. caerulea*) and willow for cricket bats was once harvested here

A last stretch of woodland alongside the railway line takes me into Stansted Mountfitchet, where my day's walk ends at the railway station. This has been a glorious day, taking me right across Hertfordshire and into Essex. April's showers have yet, in Chaucer's words, to pierce the drought of March, but I can nevertheless savour the sense of the English countryside just coming to fresh green life.

Left: Only the earthworks remain of Waytemore Castle, Bishops Stortford, constructed in 1086.

4

Stansted Mountfitchet to Saffron Walden

Through the rolling north Essex countryside to a grand house, site of a monastery dedicated to St James, and on to the town with the loveliest church in the county

All roads lead down to Stansted Mountfitchet. The village sits hunkered in a long narrow valley, which it shares with Stansted Brook and the West Anglia railway line. Look at it on a map and you'll see it is halfway down the runway of Stansted Airport, yet no planes overfly it, making it far more peaceful than you might expect. I am joined by some fellow pilgrims for the start of this stage, and we fortify ourselves for the climb out of the village with a bacon sandwich at the *Yeomans Café*, then begin our ascent. I have left Hertfordshire behind me, and now set off over north Essex's rolling hills; through a string of peaceful villages with lovely Norman churches.

I shall visit Jacobean Audley End House, a palace in all but name, built on the site of Walden Abbey. This Benedictine monastery – co-dedicated to St James, the pilgrim saint I last encountered at Ware – was erased at the Reformation, and I am keen to trace its remnants.

My destination is the town of Saffron Walden, above which the church of St Mary soars, rather as the cathedral does at Lincoln.

Bluebell wood near Stansted Mountfitchet

PRACTICAL INFORMATION

Route overview
14.2 miles (22.9km)

Following sections of the Saffron Trail and Harcamlow Way. Transport links are good on this stage and there is a good selection of places for refreshment in Stansted Mountfitchet, Newport and Saffron Walden.

An initially steep climb from Stansted Mountfitchet quickly brings you out of the village and into high country, reaching Ugley's isolated church in **3.5 miles**. A further **2.7 miles** takes you, after a dip to the River Cam, uphill again to join the Saffron Trail to Widdington. Newport, in another **2.4 miles** on the Saffron Trail, marks the rough half-way point and, with its pubs, grocery, B&B and railway station, is a good place to rest, or split the stage over two days.

Leaving Newport you follow the Harcamlow Way long-distance path for **4.4 miles** to Audley End. A final **1.2 miles**, now on the Saffron Trail once more, takes you to Saffron Walden, and the end of this stage.

Public transport options
There are **train** stations at Stansted Mountfitchet and at the midpoint of Newport. Audley End is the nearest station to Saffron Walden (1 mile away). **Bus** options include: the No 301, which calls at Stansted Mountfitchet, Newport, Audley End and Saffron Walden; and the No 59/60 between Audley End and Saffron Walden. See also public transport map and table pp29-31.

Where to eat or stay along the way
- **Stansted Mountfitchet** (see Stage 3, p61)
- **Widdington** (after 6.2 miles/10km) **Eat** at the *Fleur de Lys* pub (☎ 01799 543280, 🖥 thefleurdelys.co.uk, High St; Thur 6pm-10.30pm, Fri-Sat noon-10.30pm, Sun noon-7pm, Mon-Wed closed, food Thur 6pm-9pm, Fri & Sat noon-3pm & 6pm-9pm, Sun noon-5pm) a pleasant village local with good food.
- **Newport** (after 8.6 miles/13.9km) **Stay** at *Toll House B&B* (☎ 01799-732944 or 07946-

---

- **Terrain** Gently rolling hills, walking on footpaths and quiet lanes
- **Difficulty** Easy
- **Cumulative distance from London** 61.5 miles (99km)
- **Time** 5hrs actual walking time
- **Total ascent** 263m, 862ft
- **Map** OS Explorer *195 Braintree & Saffron Walden*
- **GPX route file & directions*** 504.pdf, 504.gpx, 504.kml at 🖥 https://trailblazer-guides.com/press * See pp27-8 for more information on downloads

484498, 🖥 thetollhouse.co.uk; Belmont Hill), a friendly B&B with good breakfasts. **Eat** at the *Coach and Horses* (☎ 01799-540292, Cambridge Rd; open Mon-Thur noon-3pm, 6pm-11pm, Fri & Sat noon-3pm & 6pm-midnight, Sun noon-9pm, food Mon-Sat noon-2pm, 6pm-9pm, Sun noon-3pm), a former coaching inn with good pub grub, 400 yds further north after route leaves the village, or rehydrate at the pleasant **drinks-only** *White Horse Inn* (☎ 01799-540002, Belmont Hill; Mon 3pm-midnight, Tue-Thur 4pm-midnight, Fri 4pm-1am, Sat noon-1am, Sun 9am-midnight.

● **Saffron Walden** Good **accommodation** options include *Cross Keys Hotel* (☎ 01799-522207, 🖥 theoldcrosskeys.co.uk; 32 High St), a lovely medieval inn with **restaurant** (Mon-Sat noon-8pm, Sun noon-5pm); and former coaching inn *Saffron Hotel* ☎ 01799-588882, 🖥 saffron-hotel.co.uk; 8-12 High St) which has good **pub grub** and Sunday roasts in its *Saffron Kitchen* (Wed & Thur 5-8.30pm, Fri & Sat noon-8.30pm, Sun noon-4.30pm, Mon & Tue closed). For a **snack** or **afternoon tea**, try *Tea Amo* (☎ 01799 529102, 🖥 teaamo.co.uk, 5 Cross St; Tue-Sun 9.30am-4pm, Mon closed;) or *Elder Street Café & Deli* (☎ 01799-543598, 🖥 elderstreet-cafedeli.co.uk, Elder St; Mon-Sat 9am-4.30pm, Sun 10am-4pm).

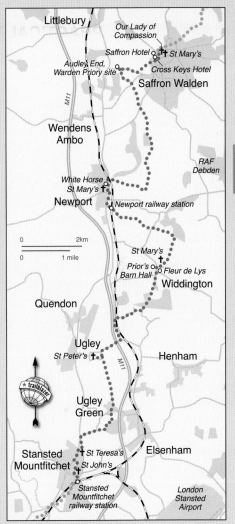

Services
● **Stansted Mountfitchet** (see Stage 3, p61)
● **Newport** For **groceries** there is a Nisa (Mon-Sat 7am-10pm, Sun 7am-7pm) on High St, or stock up on picnic supplies at **bakery** Dorington's (☎ 01799-541533, 24 High St; Mon-Fri 7am-4pm, Sat 7.30am-3.45pm, Sun closed) which does excellent sandwiches, baguettes and pastries.
● **Saffron Walden** Stock up on **picnic supplies** at Waitrose on Hill St (Mon-Sat 7am-9pm, Sun 10am-4pm) or Costcutter (daily 7am-11pm) at 41-45 High St. If you need a **laundrette** there's Launderet (☎ 07779-136495; daily 7am-9pm; 7 Emson Cl).

PILGRIMAGE HIGHLIGHTS

- **Stansted Mountfitchet** On St John's Rd is *St John the Evangelist* (☎ 01279-815243, 🖥 facebook.com/pg/St-Johns-Church-Stansted-Mountfitchet; open daily 8.30am-5.30pm, for services contact church), while *St Theresa of Lisieux* (☎ 01279-814349, 🖥 sttheresastansted.org; open at Mass times: Mon 6pm, Tue 8pm, Wed 12.30pm, Thur & Fri 9.30am, Sat 6pm, Sun 8.30am & 10am, plus 1st Sun noon) is on High Lane.
- **Ugley** *St Peter's* (☎ 01279-814285, 🖥 achurchnearyou.com/church/6407, Patmore End; open by contacting key holders ☎ 01799-543240, ☎ 01279-812263, services Sun 10am). **Pilgrim stamp in church porch.**
- **Widdington** *St Mary's* (☎ 01799-540339, 🖥 widdingtonchurch.my-free.website; Church Lane; open during services, 1st & 3rd Sun 11am, 2nd Sun 8.30am). Although not strictly a pilgrim point, on the High St *Priors Hall Barn* (☎ 0370-3331181, 🖥 english-heritage.org.uk/visit/places/priors-hall-barn, open April-Sept Sat-Sun 10am-6pm) is one of the finest surviving medieval barns in eastern England
- **Newport** *St Mary's* (☎ 01799-540339, 🖥 sites.google.com/site/smtvnw, Church St; open daily 10am-4pm, services Sun 9.30am, plus 8am on 4th Sun only).

For Saffron Walden pilgrimage highlights, see Stage 5, p88

Stansted Mountfitchet to Ugley

There are two churches on the way out of Stansted Mountfitchet. Anglican St John the Evangelist towers above the rooftops from its vantage point halfway up Chapel Hill. It's a rather forbidding Victorian statement in orange brick stratified with lines of cream stone, like a great slab of streaky bacon, its tower bristling with so many pinnacles it looks like gothic phone masts have been tacked on to it. I pass through its churchyard and out to the edge of the village, where Catholic St Theresa of Lisieux offers a complete contrast.

Above: The Church of St John the Evangelist.

This church was designed, in 2003, to evoke the great medieval granary barns of Essex. Its dedication is to a 19th century saint who died very young, at 24, from tuberculosis. By all accounts French Carmelite nun Theresa was a simple and practical soul, rather like the church that honours her. Along with Francis of Assisi, she is one of the most popular saints, and her Basilica in Lisieux, Normandy, is the second most popular place of pilgrimage in France, after Lourdes.

Inside, this is a place of coolness, calm and serenity.

Theresa loved the natural world and described herself as 'The little flower of

Above: The Church of St Theresa of Lisieux, Stansted Mountfitchet.

Jesus'. Fitting then, that as I complete the climb away from the village and into the high woods, bluebells carpet the ground.

The woodland path takes me to Ugley Green, where the track opens out onto a village green fringed with cottages – one fittingly named Arcadia – an idyllic spot just waiting for the location director of *Midsomer Murders* to come calling. The old village pump is smartly painted, the red phone box and accompanying pillar box less so.

Across the green at Fieldgate Lane a sign announces 'No Through Road'. Maybe so for motorists, but not us pilgrims. We can forge on, the lane petering out after Fieldgate Farm and a track continuing over prairie-like fields. The young wheat creates a low, green, rippling carpet to the far horizon. In the distance, eight deer walk in single file and, although

Above: Pilgrims on the trail to Ugley.

they are a good 800 yards away, they pick up our scent, pause and look our way, before ambling on.

High on this Essex prairie is Ugley Hall Farm, a little island of human habitation in an ocean of spring green. Behind the great metal barns I can just make out the brick tower of Ugley's church, St Peter's. The cows are in the dairy as I pass through the farmyard, but their lowing gives way to the cry of young lambs as I emerge on the other side, pass their nursery field and turn into the churchyard. The sheep suckling lambs in the field are echoed on the church notice board, where on a poster two lambs – looking a little more photogenic without the red numbers sprayed on their flanks – pose beneath the headline: '*I am* the good shepherd'.

St Peter's, with its 13th century rough-flint nave and

great buttressed Tudor brick tower – like a sunburned face above a pale torso – epitomises the romance of the isolated country church. The stack of car park signs in the porch are an indicator of how people flock here on special occasions.

The church was heavily restored by the Victorians, but has some lovely Burne-Jones windows of the Nativity, the Adoration of the Magi and the Flight into Egypt. In a corner is a banner, reversing the usual wording to read: 'Women's Institute Ugley'. I wonder why?

Above: The Nativity window by Edward Burne-Jones. **Below:** St Peter's Church, Ugley.

Ugley to Widdington

I say farewell to my fellow pilgrims here and continue on the farm track to a lane where I turn right to pass beneath the M11. Just before I do is a wayside stall with 'eggs from happy hens', jars of chutney in fancy red gingham bonnets, and a sign: 'Warning, this property is protected by highly trained chickens'.

Once under the M11 I turn left for the next village. The motorway is irritating me, buzzing away at my shoulder. So I'm glad that, after a half mile or so, I can turn away from it up a narrow

Widdington: The Flyr-de-lys pub (**above, left**), St Mary's Church (**right**) and village sign (**below**).

lane, duck beneath the railway and climb in zig-zags up to Little Henham, no more than a couple of farms, and into Prior's Wood, at the start of which a very reassuring sign reads 'Landowners Welcome Caring Walkers'. As we pilgrims welcome caring landowners, it sounds like a match made in heaven. In the woods I join the Saffron Trail, whose roundels bear a pink crocus in reference to the crop that once made Walden so rich that the town added 'Saffron' to its name.

Widdington to Newport

Widdington has a trio of attractions: the first I come to is the Fleur de lys, a pub painted a shade of pink so puce that it looks like it has been holding its breath for some time. Just beyond it is Prior's Hall Barn, the type of grain store from which St Theresa's in Stansted Mountfitchet takes its inspiration. It is 15th century, and a fine survivor. Four hundred oaks were felled to create it.

Third is St Mary's church. It looks entirely benign, sprawling in the sun, but a sign at the edge of the churchyard, on a slab angled to be read by anyone approaching from the village, suggests the church did not always preach about a loving God. The inscription on the slab is almost completely obscured by lichen, but I make out its message:

'Come ye children
Harken unto me
I will teach you the fear
of the Lord.'

The lichen has done a service in obscuring its message of fear, rather than love. As I read, a Union Jack is snapping away in the wind at the top of St Mary's tower, as if administering six of the best. I loop around the churchyard, where a footpath leaves the lane and takes me out over the high prairies again. The infant crop is being cowed by the sharp wind as I walk over the tops to Cabbage Wood and turn west on a farm

Above : Charming cottages in Newport, the half-way point on this stage

track to descend for Newport. My way is flanked by a wind-whipped hedgerow in which the may, the confetti-white blossom of the hawthorn, is in full flower. The old saying is 'ne're cast a clout 'til the may is out,' yet this is mid-April, and a cold one.

I have the sun in my eyes and the wind in my ears as I descend, past a newly ploughed field, its light clay soil a blonde lozenge alongside the blinding-white chalk quarries that scar the hillside.

Newport lies in a fold in the hills; a linear village strung out along the valley beside the River Cam. It has a railway station, a mini-market and bakery, two pubs and a B&B, making it an ideal spot for either lunch – for one-day walkers – or an overnight stop, if you are dividing this stage into two.

It also has a fine church – St Mary the Virgin.

ST MARY THE VIRGIN, NEWPORT

The Church of St Mary the Virgin is a treasure house. Among the highlights is the **Newport Chest** (below), a 12th century portable altar chest with oil paintings on the underside of the lid which are said to be the earliest on wood known to English art. Above the porch is a rare priest's chamber, built to house a library.

The present church is an amalgam of 13th to 16th century elements, but there is evidence of a much earlier church on this site. A fragment of a Saxon Cross has been used in the north wall.

Newport to Audley End

I left one long distance footpath – The Saffron trail – as I entered Newport and, now I am exiting it, I pick up another: the Harcamlow Way. It takes me up a valley, alongside Debden Water, a tributary of the Cam, through woods where a woodpecker is doing some drilling. A short sharp climb followed by a long, gentle descent takes me all the way to Audley End.

This is open country with the occasional wood. At one, Rosy Grove, I must duck beneath a fallen but still-growing great tree with several trunks lying across the path. Out in the open again, a yellow Tonka toy of a tractor is dwarfed by the expanse it crawls across, trailing a red pitched-roof trailer from which white powder billows over the deep green field (**below**).

The trail takes me next to a stream, shrouded beneath a swathe of thorny hedgerow, called Fulfen Slad. It's a real oddity: divided by clay dams into a series of stagnant pools, as if beavers have been at work. I imagine – in winter or after rain – the flow must resume, but in this dry spring there is no flow at all. For the last stretch to Audley End I pick up Beechy Ride, an ancient green way that takes me to Abbey Farm, once the farm to Walden Abbey, the Benedictine monastery that

stood where Audley End House is now.

Just after the farm is a place with a material link to that monastic past. On my OS map it is marked, in *ye olde* script, 'Almshouses'. From the 13th century until the Dissolution, the abbey's infirmary stood here, but for 40 years in the 17th century it was converted into an almshouse for 20 elderly servants and villagers. It consisted of a chapel, hall and kitchen built around two courtyards.

After the almshouses closed, in 1633, they were used as farm buildings. Then, in 1940s, they were given to the Anglican Diocese of Chelmsford, and used as a home for retired clergy. From the 1990s, it was run as St Mark's College, a residential youth and conference centre. But it is about to be reborn, and in a way that honours its Benedictine past. The Diocese of Chelmsford says it is to become a community in which groups of young people will 'live, learn and lead together under a shared rule of life'.

At Audley End House, in contrast, that Benedictine past has been completely obliterated and forgotten. I sense its ghost as I explore the scene of the crime.

That's not to say that what rose from the ashes of the abbey is not beautiful. Audley End House was built between 1605 and 1614 by Thomas Howard, Audley's

WALDEN ABBEY, AUDLEY END HOUSE

Walden Abbey was founded by Geoffrey de Mandeville, Earl of Essex, between 1136-44. It was dedicated to St James the Apostle and St Mary, and a site was chosen to the west of Walden, where two rivers and four roads met, to maximise its convenience for travellers and pilgrims.

Among its benefactors was Joan, Countess of Hereford who, in the 15th century, gave the abbey a gold cross containing what was said to be a fragment from the true cross. This and other treasures would have brought many pilgrims.

That history has been expunged. The abbey was dissolved and sold by Henry VIII to his Lord Chancellor, Sir Thomas Audley, but its end did not come under the Suppression of Religious Houses Acts of 1536 and 1539. Rather, it was forfeited when the abbot revealed to Thomas Cromwell that he had secretly married. The abbot argued that 'though he might not do it by the laws of men, he might do it lawfully by the laws of God for avoiding of more inconvenience'. Cromwell disagreed, and that was the end of that.

grandson, for £200,000 (£62m today). It was one of the finest Jacobean houses in England: a palace in all but name. Even today, reduced to a third of its original size, it is still imposing.

It is surrounded by parkland sculpted by Capability Brown, through which the River Cam flows. From some angles the house floats on a cloud of billowing topiary, from others it stands on a landscape designed to draw the eye right to it.

But it was built on the bones of Walden Abbey. In 1979, excavations showed that the walls of the inner court of the Jacobean house were built on the foundations of the monastic cloister. More of the abbey is thought to lie beneath the eastern lawn and flowerbeds, where Capability Brown later laid out the sumptuous parkland in which the house sits.

This is a place of plunder.

The first thing I see as I enter the great hall is a glass case holding a 16th century altarpiece, probably torn from a church in the Maastrict region, and thought to depict an exorcism. It is finely carved with great detail and shows a man prostrate on the ground, with a bishop and a friar standing over him.

I go upstairs to a series of state rooms.

The walls are lined with priceless art by Holbein, Rembrandt, Raphael and others. From 1762 the Howards, who inherited Audley End, acquired 400 paintings over three generations, a mix of Italian landscapes bought as souvenirs by those on the Grand Tour of Europe and religious scenes. There are portraits of St Catherine of Siena, a Madonna and Child, a Holy Family, Christ and the Moneylenders, St Joseph holding his flowering staff. All of them hoarded in a place built on the bones of a religious house. Ironic or what?

I move on, through a library crammed with learning; a great dining room, the table laid out for the fruit course; and down corridors lined with a string of glass cabinets housing displays of stuffed birds. There are so many, filling the cases must have emptied the skies.

Audley End to Saffron Walden
I leave the great house and walk up Audley End Rd, where I am able to duck

Above: Houses on the Audley End estate

through a gateway in the high wall surrounding the estate and cross a rise in the parkland towards the town. On this final mile an avenue of trees frames the great spire of St Mary's Church, Saffron Walden, my destination tonight. Audley End House has left me gloomy, but my spirits rise to see that great spire pricking the heavens, guiding me on to my supper, just as wayside crosses on hilltops guided medieval pilgrims.

Below: Audley End House

5

Saffron Walden
to Withersfield

Following the Harcamlow Way over
the Essex hills into Cambridgeshire,
and on into Suffolk

There is a strong Marian theme to this stage of the London to Walsingham Camino. It begins in Saffron Walden at Anglican St Mary's, which sails above Saffron Walden like a great ship in stone. Inside is a wonderful bronze depicting Mary at the moment of the Annunciation.

Tucked in St Mary's shadow is the lovely little Catholic Church of Our Lady of Compassion housed, most appropriately, in a former barn.

The Harcamlow Way footpath takes me over the hills to Church End, and the house in which the 16th-century Guild of St Mary the Virgin cared for the poor, and on from Essex into Cambridgeshire, where Bartlow's round-towered St Mary's stands close to a Roman tumuli burial site. The final St Mary's is in the Suffolk village of Withersfield, and is today's destination.

Ashdon Windmill

PRACTICAL INFORMATION

Route overview   13.8 miles (22.3km)

Following the Harcamlow Way for almost the whole route. Audley End station is a mile from the start, but the rest of the route is very rural and buses infrequent, so taxis are the most practical form of public transport. Stock up on picnic supplies in Saffron Walden as there are no shops on this stage, although there are pubs for lunch.

From Saffron Walden you follow the Harcamlow Way over gently but steadily rising ground to Church End, reached in **3.9 miles**. The Harcamlow Way continues, over undulating ground, for a final descent to Bartlow, a further **3.7 miles**. This is the rough half way point and a possible overnight stop if you are tackling this stage over two days.

It is another **3 miles** over steadily rising ground to Horseheath, still on the Harcamlow Way, after which you leave that route to follow the course of a Roman road, and then a quiet lane, for the undulating **3.2 miles** to Withersfield.

Public transport options

The start of this stage can be reached by **train** from Audley End station (1 mile from Saffron Walden) but there are no stations at any other point. **Bus** options are limited; the No 13/13A between Haverhill and Cambridge calls at Horseheath regularly, but for Withersfield it's either the SE1 community bus (pre-booking essential) or the twice-daily Star Cabs No 351 service to Haverhill. See also public transport map and table pp29-31. **Taxis** serving Withersfield include *Star Cabs* (☎ 01440-712712).

Where to eat or stay along the way

● **Saffron Walden** (see Stage 4, p75)
● **Bartlow** (after 7.7 miles, 12.4km) **Stay** and **eat** at *Three Hills gastro pub* (☎ 01223-890500, 🖳 thethreehills.co.uk, Bartlow Rd; Wed-Sat noon-11pm, Sun noon-5pm, closed Mon & Tue; food Wed-Sat noon-2pm & 6pm-9pm, Sun noon-4pm,) 17th-century pub with highly-regarded restaurant and six en-suite rooms.
● **Horseheath** (after 10.6 miles/17km) *The Old Red Lion* (☎ 01223-892909, 🖳 theoldredlion.co.uk, Linton Rd; Mon-Thur noon-9pm, Fri & Sat noon-10.30pm, Sun noon-6pm, food Mon-Sat noon-2.30pm & 5-8pm, Sun noon-4pm) is a village local with **pub grub** and **accommodation**. Another option to **stay** here is *Chequer Cottage B&B* (☎ 01223-891522, Streetly End) which has a garden room annexe in country setting, 400yds off the route.

● **Terrain** Footpaths   ● **Difficulty** Moderate
● **Cumulative distance from London** 75.3miles, 121.3km
● **Time** 5hrs actual walking time   ● **Total Ascent** 316m, 1037ft
● **Maps** OS Explorer *195 Braintree & Saffron Walden; 210 Newmarket & Haverhill*
● **GPX route file & directions*** 505.pdf, 505.gpx, 505.kml at 🖳 https://trailblazer-guides.com/press * See pp27-8 for more information on downloads

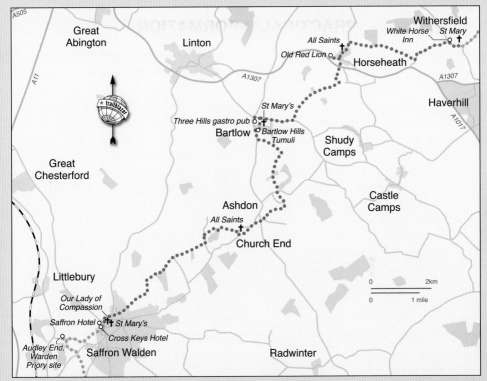

- **Withersfield** *White Horse Inn* (☎ 01440-706081 , 💻 withersfieldwhitehorse.co.uk, Hollow Hill, Mon 5-9pm, Tue-Thur noon-3pm & 6-10/11pm, Fri & Sat noon-11pm, Sun noon-7pm, food Mon 5-8pm, Tue-Sat noon-2pm & 6pm-9pm, Sun noon-4pm) is a popular village inn with good pub **food** and en-suite **accommodation.**
- **Haverhill** (2 miles/3.2km off-route from the junction of Stages 5 and 6) offers a range of **accommodation** including: *Rosebarne Bed and Breakfast* (☎ 01440-708784, 💻 rosebarne.weebly.com; 5 rms), conveniently placed on the road into town at 162 Withersfield Rd; the *Suffolk Hotel and Nine Jars* (☎ 01440-711998, 💻 ninejars.co.uk, 9 High St; 8 rms) in the town centre, with restaurant and bar; or chain hotel *Travelodge* (💻 travelodge.co.uk) on Phoenix Rd.

Services
- **Saffron Walden** (see Stage 4, p75)
- **Horseheath** There is a Post Office here but with limited opening hours: *Horseheath Post office and Tangent Gifts* (☎ 01223-897960, 💻 horseheathpostoffice.business.site, West Wickham Rd; open Mon-Tue 9am-noon, Wed-Thur closed, Fri 9am-noon, Sat-Sun closed).
- **Haverhill** has **supermarkets**: *Sainsbury's* (Mon-Sat 7.30am-10pm, Sun 10am-4pm; Haycocks Rd) and *Aldi* (Mon-Sat 8am-10pm, Sun 10am-4pm; Lordscroft Ln) plus a **laundrette** at 40 Queen St *Anglia Laundrette* (💻 mywashing.co.uk/Haverhill; daily 7am-9pm).

PILGRIMAGE HIGHLIGHTS

● **Saffron Walden** *St Mary's* (☎ 01799-506024, 🖥 stmaryssaffronwalden.org, Church Path; open daily, check with church for hours, services Sun 8am, 10am & 11.45am, for weekdays see website). *Our Lady of Compassion* (🖥 olcsaffron-walden.org.uk, Castle St; open at Mass times, Mon-Fri 9am, Sat 6pm, Sun 8.30am, 10.30am). The *Turf Maze* is actually a labyrinth (🖥 visitsaffronwalden .gov.uk/2020/02/turf-maze-labyrinth, 3 Chaters Hill; open at all times) and offered an alternative for those who could not go on a conventional pilgrimage
● **Church End** *All Saints* (☎ 01799-584171, 🖥 allsaintsashdon.org.uk, open daylight hours, services Sun 9.30am, Church Hill). *Guildhall of St Mary the Virgin* is now a private house, can be viewed from the churchyard.
● **Bartlow** *St Mary's* (🖥 achurchnearyou.com/church/13808, Little Linton; open daily 10am-4pm, check with church for services). **Pilgrim stamp in church.**
● **Horseheath** *All Saints* (☎ 01799-585977, 🖥 achurchnearyou.com/church/13817, West Wickham Rd; open contact keyholders on noticeboard, services 3rd Sun 10am).
For Withersfield pilgrim highlights, see Stage 6, p100

St Mary's Church

Saffron Walden

Everywhere I walk in Saffron Walden the spire of St Mary's watches over me. It looms round corners, peers over rooftops, is glimpsed down alleys, and keeps a keen eye on everything that goes on in the town.

I've planned my arrival so I can start at St Mary's and take in the town on the evening I get here, and then in the morning go to Mass at Our Lady of Compassion before setting out on the next stage of my pilgrimage.

St Mary's

Representations of the saffron crocus, grown here extensively for 400 years until the late 18th century, appear on the roof and above arches in St Mary's, which is as imposing inside as out. Walking up the great nave, a cathedral-sized space 50ft high and 108ft long, I suddenly get the urge to sing. The present church dates from the 13th century, but there has probably been a church asserting its spiritual

Above – Saffron Walden: Sumptuous gold in Our Lady of Compassion (**left**). **Centre and right**: A copy Correggio's *Madonna and Child with St Jerome* and the rood cross at St Mary's.

dominance from this spot since Saxon times. It was rebuilt in the 16th century by master masons who also worked on Eton and Kings College, Cambridge, and the 193-foot-tall spire was added in 1831.

I leave St Mary's to explore the town. Saffron Walden has a powerful medieval feel. On the corner of High St and King St is The Cross Keys, a 15th century inn that will have hosted pilgrims along with secular clients, and where I am staying. Up King St is The Rows, the shopping district from medieval times. Then comes the Market Square, where markets have been held on Tuesdays and Saturdays since the 13th century.

In its centre is what I mistake for a holy or market cross, until I learn it is actually a Victorian drinking fountain, dating from 1863. No matter, high on each of its four stone faces is a sculpted, high relief scene from the book of Exodus. Each features Moses and show him: liberating the children of Israel from slavery in Egypt; about to kill an Egyptian who is smiting a Hebrew labourer; helping Reul's daughters to water their father's flock; and leading the He-

brews out of Egypt in the Exodus. It is by John Francis Bentley, a convert to Catholicism who designed Westminster Cathedral.

I carry on to The Common, to walk what is known as the Turf Maze but which is actually a labyrinth, the difference being that while a maze is designed to confuse, with deceptive turns and dead ends, a labyrinth follows one true path to the centre, and hence has a clear connection with pilgrimage. The path it offers may appear to be taking you away from your goal at times but, stick with it, and you will reach your destination.

This ancient labyrinth, with 17 circuits, is the largest of its kind in the world, and one of only eight to survive in England. Some cathedrals feature labyrinths marked out in the tiles of the floor, notably Chartres, and walking them offered a symbolic path of pilgrimage for those unable to travel to shrines such as Walsingham, Santiago or Rome.

I walk back to my hotel via Church St, and the 14th century, former Old Sun Inn. It is a fine example of the tradition of covering a timber framed building with a

THE MARIAN SHRINE AT ST MARY'S

A highlight of St Mary's is the north chapel which, by rights, ought to be called the Lady Chapel, given it contains a 200-year-old copy of Correggio's 16th century *Madonna and Child with St Jerome*, and a bronze sculpture of Mary called *Magnificat*.

'Magnificat' is the opening word of Mary's song of praise in Latin, which runs, in translation: 'My soul magnifies the Lord, and my spirit rejoices in God my Saviour'. This statue was made by sculptor and parishioner Tessa Hawkes, and portrays Mary 'as a young and vulnerable woman, receiving the news from the Angel Gabriel that she is to be the mother of Jesus, God's Son.'

A notice alongside explains that during its creation the sculpture 'took on a life of its own'. Tessa's original intention had been for Mary's arms to be outstretched, as if she were asking: 'Why me?' and for her back to be 'bent and vulnerable' but, overnight, her arms dropped and her back straightened. It was as if she was finding the strength to fulfil the remarkable role Gabriel assigned her. So it was no longer a case of 'why me?' but of 'thy will be done'.

Below: The Turf Maze, Saffron Walden

Above: Pargeting on the former Sun Inn

skim of plaster that is then decorated with a sort of bas relief pattern, a process known as pargeting. Two mythical figures are depicted, who may represent the giants Gog and Magog, or Tom Hickathrift, a giant-killing figure from East Anglian folklore, and the Wisbech Giant he thwarted.

Next morning begins with Mass at Our Lady of Compassion, reached via an alley from the churchyard of St Mary's. It presents an anonymous, orange-brick face to Castle St, but inside is a revelation. It feels like a hall house, far grander than the 17th century barn it was in a former life, with black timbers spidering the white plaster walls and windows set high above my head. The other theme is that of gold. Above the sanctuary is a ceiling in deep

blue dotted with gold stars; the simple screen-like reredos glisters with it, as do the points of the crucifix. Most golden of all is the soaring cover to the tabernacle, delicate tracery topped with an angel. For some reason the image comes to me of finding a golden egg in a magpie's nest.

Saffron Walden to Church End

I pass Walsingham House as I leave Our Lady of Compassion. In fact it is named after a local family, rather than my destination, but seeing the name seems like a good omen as I set out.

It is a steady climb out of town, but quickly achieved, and I soon emerge on open, rising ground with Saffron Walden tucked in the valley behind me. I shall be following the Harcamlow Way to Horseheath, my lunch stop. The oil seed rape (**below**) is flowering early this dry spring, and already a knee-high ocean of yellow spreads around me as I approach Little Grimsditch Wood, come out to pass Butler's Farm, and continue on a track that, curiously, is a seam of chalk over fields of terracotta speckled with tiny green wheat shoots. A herd of a dozen or more deer are munching the crop in the distance to my

right. Oh how the farmers must love them.

The spike of All Saints, rising from its flint tower above the trees ahead, tells me I am approaching Church End, a place of worship dating back to pagan times.

Church End to Bartlow

In the 14th century, perhaps because of the Black Death, the village moved down the valley to Ashdon, and is now in two parts. Church End, a hamlet of a few cottages and church grouped around the green, stands on the lip of the River Bourne valley.

The present All Saints is 11th century, and replaced a pre-Conquest wooden building, which may in turn have replaced a pagan temple. It is an oddly mismatched building, but no less charming for that. Beyond the 14th century western tower, with its gnarled oak door, comes the modest nave, followed by a spacious chancel flanked on the south side by a large chapel. The narrow lancet windows of the nave are pinpricks compared to the great square window in the chapel, which would not look out of place in a Tudor palace. It's as if a ballroom has been tacked onto a cottage.

Across the graveyard from the church is a remarkable old building: the Guildhall of St Mary the Virgin. The timber-framed house is first mentioned in 1501 when it was left to the charitable guild in a will. In 1731 it was divided into three homes for poor families, and only became one house again in the 20th century.

I slip out at the bottom of the churchyard and into the valley, crossing a stream and skirting Ashdon before climbing again, towards the windmill that is glinting white in the sun. All Saints dominates the hill behind me, the windmill the one ahead, like a snub-nosed bullet placed on end, with a twirling bow-tie under its chin.

Above: All Saints, Church End.

I pass it and drop down again through expansive fields to a grand house: Ashdon Place, like a feudal fiefdom in its cloistered valley. For some reason the Harcamlow Way signs have been removed from this stretch of the path, but I get used to spotting the darker circles on posts from which the roundels have been swiped.

The route runs up an avenue to the east of the grand house and cluster of farm buildings, past a filly and foal in a field, through Home Wood and over expansive fields once again. Here, I am happy to see that an infant hedgerow, the saplings protected in a double row of plastic tubing, has been planted to replace an ancient one that has been grubbed out, righting a wrong.

On the outskirts of Bartlow I pass from Essex into Cambridgeshire, the path running above the lane into the village, taking me to the curious Bartlow Hills Tumuli.

In a clearing in the wood rise three conical mounds, like three anthills 45ft high. I scramble up the first and, at tree-top height, look across at the other two.

There is another treasure in Bartlow: my first round tower church of the pilgrimage. I shall see more as I get into Suffolk and Norfolk, but these often-Saxon treasures are rare in Cambridgeshire.

This church, another dedicated to Mary, is a gem. The circular west tower is

thought to be all that remains of the original 11th or early 12th-century church, the nave being a mere stripling from the 14th century.

The tower is faced with tiny pebbles, mostly a pale gold but with a wide band of dark grey at head height, like a tide mark. Inside, fragments of 15th century wall paintings have been uncovered, with depictions of St Christopher, St Michael weighing souls, and St George's dragon, but not the saint himself. In a niche is a simple touch that shows how loved this church is: a white jug of daffodils stands beside a crucifix. In the countryside they have expired, making way for bluebells, but here a carefully selected bunch, from solid yellow to cream with an orange inner trumpet, shine brightly.

Bartlow, with its gastro-pub-with rooms, is an ideal place for lunch, or to split the stage if you are covering it over two days.

Above: St Mary's Church, Bartlow, with its circular tower and dragon wall painting.

Bartlow to Horseheath

A short stretch along a quiet lane takes me out once more into high country. Two pheasants whir away, taking off with a sound like a motorbike and an old-fashioned football rattle. This exceptionally dry spring has left the land parched. The fields are gritty deserts under a hot sun in a cobalt blue sky. Towards Horseheath, the path takes on a green-way feel, winding through thick hedgerows where the may is out and the bees are busy, and the sulphur yellow butterflies wheel around in skittish flight.

I hit my first big road of the day, the A1307 at Horseheath, but thankfully it's quiet. I cross to the blessedly-bypassed village, with its pub, the Red Lion, post office and church. All Saints' – 600 years old, with Norman fragments – has an unusual 16th century sundial above the porch door. It is angled, cut into the church wall on the left, presumably to align it with the sun, and the hand is a saw.

BARTLOW HILLS TUMULI

The Romans established a large military camp here, and a wealthy community grew up from the 1st to the 4th centuries. Once there were seven of these curious mounds (a fourth survives on private land) which are Romano-British burial sites. The three accessible ones are known as The Three Hills.

For centuries, local folklore held that these were the graves of those killed at the Battle of Ashingdon, or Assundun, which may have taken place near Saffron Walden in 1016, against Danish invaders. But, in the 19th century, excavation showed they were the graves of a wealthy Romano-British family and date from the 1st or 2nd centuries. Valuable burial offerings, including decorated bronze vessels, glass, pottery and large wooden chests were discovered, plus an altar under the largest mound. A Roman villa stood to the north.

Horseheath to Withersfield

I pick up a Roman road just outside Horseheath for the final stage to Withersfield, where the inn will be my resting place for the night. The old road runs north west to south east, with Cambridge to my left, and Haverhill to my right. Walsingham pilgrims from Cambridge will have joined the route here.

After descending gently on the Roman road, with Haverhill in the valley ahead of me, I cut left over fields, through woods, and join a lane via Silver St to reach the White Horse Inn on the outskirts of Withersfield. A little further on, past a string of whitewashed thatched cottages, is another church dedicated to St Mary the Virgin, where this stage ends. I go in to pay my respects, then return to the inn, where my pilgrim-sized appetite is sated, and I sleep an untroubled sleep.

Below: Desert-dry fields after Bartlow

6
Withersfield to Stansfield

A meditative amble through bucolic Suffolk countryside

This is the first of two gentle rural stages through peaceful Suffolk landscapes, beneath vast, ever-changing skies. There are no great pilgrim towns along the way, rather a string of beautiful, quiet villages with lovely medieval churches, welcoming inns and even the odd shop. There is also a priory disguised as a farm.

Between villages, the Camino route follows green ways and quiet lanes in a landscape that is quintessentially English, linking communities whose proud traditions are reflected in the handsome village signs on each green that I pass. These are careful records of local crafts and legends, and I find I am collecting them, rather like Panini stickers, mentally pasting each one in my pilgrim album as I pass.

Approaching Stansfield

6

PRACTICAL INFORMATION

Route overview   12.2 miles (19.7km)

This stage is deep in the countryside with little in the way of buses or services along the way, although there is a good pub and a village shop (open mornings only) at Hundon, the halfway point. Note that at the time of research the pub in Stansfield was closed pending new ownership, so until it reopens, options to stay overnight are either a mile before or a mile after the end of this stage, or take a taxi to Bury St Edmunds.

The route begins with a **2.5-mile** stretch, first climbing gently but steadily, then descending similarly, over quiet lanes to Great Wratting. There is a further climb and descent to Hundon (**4.8 miles**), where this stage could be divided.

From Hundon it is **2.1 miles** on footpaths, ascending steadily to Chipley Abbey Farm, site of Chipley Priory. The final stretch is a steady descent, followed by a short up-hill section for Stansfield, reached in another **2.8 miles**.

Public transport options

This stage is very rural with no stations and limited bus services. Withersfield is linked with Haverhill (3 miles away) by the twice-daily Star Cabs No 351 **bus** or SE1 community bus (pre-booking essential) which can also call in Great Wratting, Hundon and Stansfield by arrangement. The No 14/15 to Bury St Edmunds calls in Great Wratting and the No 59/60 connects Haverhill with Saffron Walden. See also public transport map and table pp29-31.

Taxis serving Withersfield, Hundon and Stansfield include *Star Cabs* (☎ 01440-712712) and *Sudbury Cab Company* (☎ 01787-373222, 🖳 sudburycab.co.uk).

Where to eat or stay along the way

● **Withersfield/Haverhill** (see Stage 5, p87)
● **Great Wratting** (after 2.5 miles/4km) *The Red Lion* (☎ 01440-783237, 🖳 facebook.com/wrattingredlion, School Rd; Mon-Thur 11am-3pm & 5.30pm-10pm, Fri- Sun 11am-10pm, food daily noon-1.45pm & 6.30-8.30pm).
● **Hundon** (after 7.3 miles/11.7km) **Eat** at the *Rose and Crown* (☎ 01440-786261, 🖳 hundon-village.co.uk/roseandcrown.html, North St; Tue 6pm-10pm, Wed-Thur noon-2pm, 6pm-11pm, Fri-Sat noon-12pm, Sun noon-9pm, food hours contact pub).

● **Terrain** Gently rolling hills
● **Difficulty** Easy
● **Cumulative distance from London** 87.5miles (141km)
● **Time** 4hrs 20mins actual walking time
● **Total ascent** 328m/1076ft
● **Map** OS Explorer 210 *Newmarket & Haverhill*
● **GPX route file & directions*** 506.pdf, 506.gpx, 506.kml at 🖳 https://trailblazer-guides.com/press * See pp27-8 for more information on downloads

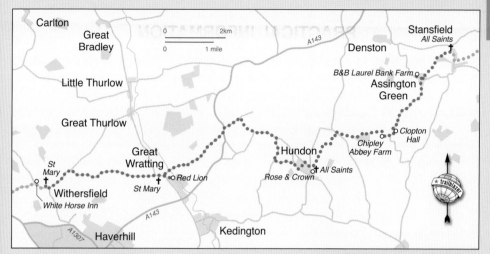

If dividing this stage here, the options to **stay** are a little off the route: there's the *Plough,* (☎ 01440-786789, 🖳 facebook.com/The-Plough-Inn-Hundon, Brockley Green; open Mon 6pm-11pm, Tue-Fri noon-3pm & 6pm-10pm, Sat noon-10pm Sun noon-8pm, food hours contact pub) 1.8 miles/2.9km off route; or *Suffolk retreats* (☎ 0845-5213313, 07947-187073, 🖳 suffolkretreats.co.uk, Hundon Grange) yurts, minimum 2 nights stay, 1 mile/1.6km off route.

● **Assington Green** (after 11.2 miles/18.1km) *Laurel Bank Farm B&B* (☎ 01284-789279, 🖳 suffolksbedandbreakfast.co.uk) offers bed, breakfast and evening meals, is 200yds off the route and – at 1 mile, 1.6km short of the destination, the closest accommodation to the end of this stage.

● **Stansfield** At the time of research Stansfield's pub, *Stansfield Compasses* (☎ 01284-789263, 🖳 stansfieldcompasses.co.uk, High St) was closed pending new ownership. Until it reopens there is nowhere to stay in Stansfield itself but see Stage 7 p108 for accommodation at Hawkedon, 1.2 miles/1.9km further on.

Services
● **Hundon** On North St is the*Village Shop and Post Office* (☎ 01440-786223; Mon-Sat 9am-1pm)

Right: Village sign, Withersfield

PILGRIMAGE HIGHLIGHTS

- **Withersfield** *St Mary the Virgin* (☎ 01440-763080 (church office), ☎ 01440-710077 (church warden); 🖳 achurchnearyou.com/church/2121, Church St; open daily 8am-8pm, services 1st & 3rd Sun, 4pm). **Pilgrim stamp in church.**
- **Great Wratting** *St Mary's* (☎ 01440-762901, 🖳 achurchnearyou.com/church/2122, Withersfield Rd; not left open, but keyholder in Old Rectory next door, services check website).
- **Hundon** *All Saints* (☎ 01787-277515, 🖳 achurchnearyou.com/church/2126, North St; open daily 10am-3pm, services 2nd Sun 9am, 4th Sun 4pm). **Pilgrim stamp in church.**

For pilgrim highlights in Stansfield, see Stage 7, page 110

Withersfield

There be dragons in Withersfield. A pair of them, coiled on the 13th century door handle at St Mary's. They look a little tortoise-like with their oval bodies, but no matter, they make opening the door to this lovely church a pleasure in itself.

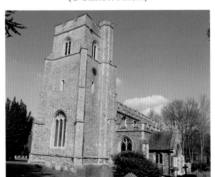

Above: Dragons on the door handle, St Mary's Withersfield (© Simon Knott)

Inside is a remarkable selection of illustrated (meaning carved) pew ends. I see St Michael holding a scale, on one side of which sits a sinner, on the other – represented by an evil, Golum-like creature – his sins. The man holds a rosary, which would have been frowned upon post-Reformation.

Elsewhere, a tiny St George slays a very large dragon, and two beasts, maybe bears, fight among what look like grape vines.

Above: St Mary's Withersfield

On other benches are a swan, a mermaid and a pelican. The pelican is a symbol of piety in Christian tradition because, according to legend, the mother will feed her young on her own blood, symbolising Christ's sacrificial death and resurrection.

Withersfield to Great Wratting

I leave crenellated St Mary's, sitting high above the lane through the village, and reach the village green, where I mentally stick the first village sign in my collection. This one depicts the harvesting of osiers, the young, green and flexible shoots of willow used in basket weaving. One rustic-looking fellow cuts them while another pitchforks them into a cart. A maiden

Above: A row of thatched cottages in Withersfield

stands, one hand on hip, the other on a pitchfork, in an 'I'm a little teapot' pose.

The bustling town of Haverhill is just to the south, but keeps itself to itself, and the early-morning lanes are deserted as I turn north up Turnpike Hill, and out of the village. It is a steady but gentle climb past Paradise Farm before a drop down to the next village, Great Wratting, which lies in the valley of the River Stour.

This is a pattern I shall enjoy all day: of villages tucked into the valleys, wide open farmland on the rises in between. It sets up a rhythm in the walk that suits me well: long periods for reflection in nature, short bursts of village life, with church for sustenance and pub for spiritual succour. Or have I got that the wrong way round?

Above: St Mary's Church, Great Wratting

In Great Wratting, I find another St Mary's, like its sister in Withersfield stand-

ing tall on a rise above the lane through the village. I climb the path through the handsome lychgate and read a quotation in the porch that seems to have pilgrims in mind. It begins:

'Christ whose true temple is not made with hands
Guide questing feet that find this place of prayer'.

Inside this large flint church, 13th century but with Saxon roots and a Victorian makeover, there is a mix of ancient and modern. The rood screen between chancel and nave is early 20th century, possibly a gift from William Henry Smith, son of the founder of stationers W H Smith and one-time local resident. The curve of the medieval stairs that once led to the rood loft over the original screen, where the rood cross or crucifix stood, is visible in the wall behind the pulpit, and there is a *sedilia*, a set of three stone seats for priest and assistants, of a similar age.

The village clusters around the River Stour, and the ford that crosses it is great for wild swimming. A sign warns me I am forbidden from washing my car in the waters. No mention of pilgrim feet.

I wonder about the village's name. Was Great Wratting once renowned as a great place to catch rats? No. Wratting, I learn from the parish council's website, comes partly from 'wreat', the medieval name for madder. I read: 'Madder was crucial to our ancestors as a dyeing agent, the only real source of the colour red, and it was to Great Wratting that early medieval East Anglians would come when they wanted to wear or sell red clothes.'

The village sign (**left**), a handsome design in painted oak beneath a miniature thatched roof, which stands on the green opposite St Mary's, includes the pale-yellow star-like flowers of Madder, along with a plough and sack of corn.

Above and below:
All Saints Church, Hundon

Great Wratting to Hundon

I climb out of the Stour Valley, up through the corn fields to what counts as the tops. Opposite Barnardiston School I leave the lanes for a spell on a track that runs south east, dead-straight, between high hedgerows. It's called Borley Lane but is unsurfaced, and I have it to myself as I stride on, the sun in my face. The country opens up, the fields stretched over the flank of the hills. The tall stone tower of All Saints, peeking above the horizon, guides me towards Hundon, hidden in its valley. I descend via Chimney St and Babel Green, where a trio of beautifully groomed horses follow me companionably, me on my side of the fence, they on theirs.

As I pass the village school I hear the children, immersed in their lessons, raising a happy murmur like busy bees. This pillar of the community forms a triangle with the two other essentials of the healthy village trinity: church and pub. The latter two make Hundon a perfect lunch stop, or point at which to end the day, if you are splitting this stage into two.

I visit All Saints church first, the clock in the flint and dressed-stone tower ticking slowly, deeply along like a steady, healthy

Left: Attracting local interest while passing Babel Green

heartbeat. I tip my head back to see the top of that high tower, where the stair turret climbs a good storey above it, and ends in a wooden bellcote sheltering the great bell, surmounted by a peacock weathervane.

It's a lovely, clearly much-loved place, shaped almost organically over three centuries – 14th to 16th – and then, tragically, destroyed by fire in 1914. But it was rebuilt during wartime, faithfully to the original.

I stop and admire the time-battered, two-storey 15th century porch (**below**), and the way the white wooden slats over the doors imitate tied-back curtains, urging me to enter. I am reminded that church porches were designed as places of refuge, hospitality and community, where parishioners could hold meetings, and where strangers and pilgrims might find shelter.

Inside, all is plain and simple, and I sit and listen to that clock – the heartbeat of the place – and sense my own heart slowing to match its sober beat. Pilgrimage is

CHIPLEY PRIORY

Chipley Priory was an Augustinian house, founded some time before 1235, and dedicated to the Blessed Virgin. It was one of a string of Augustinian hostelries on the pilgrim path from London to Walsingham. I encountered the first way back at Waltham Abbey and, as I get closer to Walsingham, others will be on my path, including at Brandon.

This was not a grand monastery, and it failed before Henry VIII was able to get his hands on it. In 1291 its annual income was less than £5, or £5,800 today.

By 1455 the buildings were in ruins and, in 1468, the Bishop of Norwich allowed a college for priests 3½ miles south at Stone-next-Clare, (now Stone-by-Clare), to take over the land. Its successor, Stoke College, is a co-educational day school.

In the 17th century, the present farmhouse was built from material scavenged from the priory. The priory church was destroyed, probably in 1818, and artefacts including a bell, a stone coffin, and human remains were taken to St Mary the Virgin, Poslingford, a village 1½ miles south.

held precious in this church. The rector, Revd Mark Woodrow, is a Priest Associate of the Shrine of Our Lady of Walsingham, members of which promise, among other things, to 'promote devotion to Our Lady and pilgrimage to Walsingham'.

The *Rose and Crown* is virtually next door and, twice awarded community pub of the year by CAMRA, is a welcoming place for lunch. There is a village shop and post office, too, just up the road, where I stock up on pilgrim treats before taking the footpath that runs through the churchyard and on up the Stour valley.

Hundon to Chipley Priory

The footpath climbs towards Hundon Hall, the fields a mix of stumps of corn stalks like a thatch seen at a narrow angle, and great acres of newly-drilled and just-emerging green shoots, like a close-up of Wayne Rooney's hair implants.

On a rise is a curious thing, a great fake tree hiding a mobile-phone mast. It looks, with its stubby arms and spiky top, less

like a tree, more like a brown, petrified version of one of those air-inflated figures that dance around wildly on roadsides, promoting businesses desperate to attract passing trade.

Just past the hall a green way, Black Grove Lane, takes me on its muddy route through Black Grove Plantation and on to a farm that hides a priory. These days it is

called Chipley Abbey Farm and is formed from the ruins of Chipley Priory. My OS Explorer map tells me that the fishponds still exist, and I glimpse brackish water through the trees in the private gardens, but no other evidence remains of what was once a pilgrim refuge.

Chipley Priory to Stansfield

My path runs through the farmyard and out to a lane, where I turn left and pass Clopton Hall, also built with material recycled from the priory. The hall wears a great arch of hedge like a droopy moustache before its front door, and the render covering its 16th century walls is painted a deep pink, making it look like a very angry moustachioed man.

Above: Clopton Hall, constructed using recycled materials from Chipley Priory.

From here I follow the quietest of lanes, on another upland slope, the grass growing undisturbed by traffic on its meridian, proclaiming this a walkers' road.

From Assington Green I leave the quiet lane and take a footpath again, on a long slow descent to the valley of the River Glem, and then a climb through woods up Plough Hill to Glebe Farm, where I spot an unusual gate latch: a horseshoe, fixed at a point just off centre, so that it can easily be swung to catch a loop on the gate and keep it closed. Genius.

The path delivers me to the churchyard of All Saints', Stansfield, and the peaceful end to the most relaxed and contemplative stage of my pilgrimage so far.

7

Stansfield to Bury St Edmunds

Over the 'Hill of the Hawks' to the great pilgrim town of Bury St Edmunds, home to England's one-time patron saint

The approach to one of England's most important medieval shrines is one of mounting anticipation, and speeds my tired legs. At Bury St Edmunds I shall be half-way to Walsingham, and I am relishing my arrival at that key pilgrim staging post.

I walk in the footsteps of many pilgrims: commoners, nobility, royalty, but am reminded, as I am about to set out from All Saints in Stansfield, that this is also a lovely walk, and not to be rushed. As I sit in the church porch, a lady walking her greyhound asks me where I am headed, and when I say 'Bury', she asks which route. I run off the villages: Hawkedon, Rede, Whepstead, and she nods approval at each one, and asks if I am going via footpaths. I say I am and she says I will have a lovely walk.

She is right. I do. And, as I press deeper into Suffolk, I savour a further succession of charming Norman churches, one of them unique in its dedication to St Petronilla, another where it is possible to piece together fragments of the shattered pilgrim tradition that once thrived along my path.

Passing Stansfield Church

PRACTICAL INFORMATION

ROUTE OVERVIEW   12.2 miles (19.7km)

There are no shops on this stage until Bury St Edmunds. Whepstead is the halfway point and has a pub for lunch but no accommodation – if dividing this section here you could take a bus or taxi to Bury St Edmunds for the night, then back the next day.

There is, broadly, a gentle but sustained climb over the first half of the stage, and a similar descent for the second. From Stansfield it is a short hop between valleys to Hawkedon, reached in **1.2 miles**. A further **2.5 miles** takes you via a green way and footpaths to the next village, Rede. It is then **3 miles**, mainly along quiet lanes, to Whepstead, a good point to pause for lunch, or split the stage into two day-walks.

From Whepstead the route follows the Bury to Clare Walk. There are no more villages on the way to Bury, but the hamlet of Pinford End is reached in **1.9 miles**. In a further **1.4 miles** the route leaves the Bury to Clare Walk and joins the St Edmund Way. This path takes you right in to the city, reached in **2.2 miles**.

Public transport options

This is another very rural stage, with only the end point at Bury St Edmunds accessible by **train**. There are occasional buses, but taxis are the best option for joining or leaving the route before Bury. The SE1 community **bus** (pre-booking essential) can call in Stansfield and Rede by arrangement, and the infrequent No 374 stops in Whepstead en route between Clare and Bury St Edmunds. See also public transport map and table pp29-31. **Taxis** include *Star Cabs* (☎ 01440-712712), *Sudbury Cab Company* (☎ 01787-373222, 🖳 sudburycab.co.uk) and in Bury St Edmunds, *A1 Cars* (☎ 01284-766777, 🖳 a1cars.co.uk).

Where to eat or stay along the way

● **Stansfield** (see Assington Green, Stage 6, p99).

● **Hawkedon** (after 1.2 miles / 1.9km) **Stay** and **eat** at the lovely 15th-century *Queens Head* (☎ 01284-789218, 🖳 hawkedonqueen.co.uk, Rede Rd; open Mon-Thur 5pm-11pm, Fri-Sun noon-11pm, food Wed-Thur 6pm-9pm, Fri-Sun noon-2.30/3pm & 6pm-9pm), a free house with restaurant-quality menu. Accommodation is in a medieval hall and former stables.

● **Rede** (after 3.6 miles / 5.8km) The *Plough Inn* (☎ 01284-789208, 🖳 facebook.com then search Plough Inn Rede; open Tue-Sun 11am-3pm & 6.30pm-11pm) is a 15th century pub on The Green, with good **food** and garden.

● **Whepstead** (after 6.8 miles / 10.9km then 1 mile / 1.6km off route) Take a short detour for **lunch** at the *White Horse* (☎ 01284-735760, 🖳 thewhitehorsewhepstead.pub, Rede

---

● **Terrain** Footpaths and quiet lanes   ● **Difficulty** Easy / Moderate
● **Cumulative distance from London** 99.7miles (160.7km)
● **Time** 4hrs 15mins actual walking time   ● **Total ascent** 178.5m (568ft)
● **Maps** OS Explorer *210 Newmarket & Haverhill, 211 Bury St Edmunds & Stowmarket*
● **GPX route file & directions*** 507.pdf, 507.gpx, 507.kml at 🖳 https://trailblazer-guides.com/press * See pp27-8 for more information on downloads

Rd; open Wed-Sat noon-11pm, Sun noon-8pm, food Wed-Fri noon-2.30 & 5pm-8.30pm, Sat noon-8.30pm, Sun noon-5pm).

● **Bury St Edmunds Stay** at the historic four-star *Angel Hotel* (☎ 01284-714000, 🖥 theangel.co.uk; 3 Angel Hill) opposite Abbey Gardens; or reliable chain hotel *Premier Inn* (🖥 premierinn.com; Raingate St). **Food** options include *Pilgrim's Kitchen* (☎ 01284-748738, Angel Hill; 8am-4/5pm) a good lunch spot by the cathedral, and *Abbey Gardens Café* (☎ 01284 758380; Mustow St; 10/11am-4/5pm, winter closed), great for coffee and cake.

Services

● **Bury St Edmunds** has **supermarkets** Waitrose (Mon-Sat 7.30am-8pm, Sun 10am-4pm) on Robert Boby Way and Tesco Express (daily 6am-11pm; 24-26 Cornhill). There are also two **laundrettes**: The Coin Op Laundrette (☎ 01284-361386; daily 8am-6pm) at 10 Hardwick Shopping Centre on Home Farm Ln; or Wash-And-Spin (☎ 07862-712041, 30 Cadogan Rd; 7am-6pm).

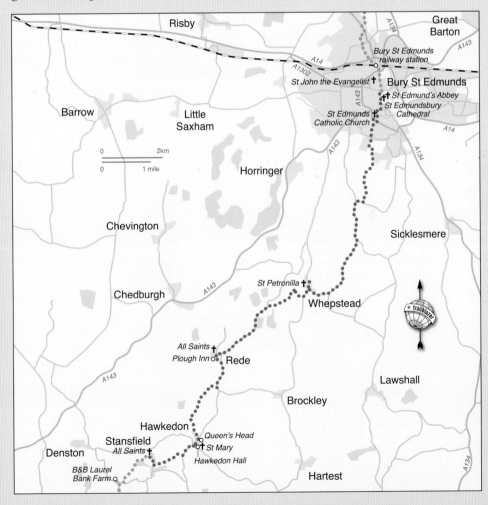

PILGRIMAGE HIGHLIGHTS

- **Stansfield** *All Saints* (☎ 07815-441304, 🖥 bansfieldbenefice.org.uk/services, open for services, refer to website) is on Plough Hill.
- **Hawkedon** *St Mary* (☎ 01284-850857, 🖥 achurchnearyou.com/church/2114; open 10am-4pm, services 2nd Sun 9am, 4th Sun 10.45am). **Pilgrim stamp in church.**
- **Rede** *All Saints* (☎ 01284 850078, 🖥 achurchnearyou.com/church/2113, Church Cl; open 10am-4pm, for services contact church).
- **Whepstead** *St Petronilla* (☎ 01284-830322, 🖥 achurchnearyou.com/church/2210, Church Hill; open daylight hours, for services contact church).

For details of pilgrim highlights in Bury St Edmunds, see Stage 8, page 120

Stansfield

The stone benches that line the porch at All Saints, Stansfield were once perched upon by members of the parish council while they discussed village business. Today they provide a useful place for a pilgrim to gather their thoughts before setting off for the day. The morning sun is angling in and warming me and those mellow stones. There is an ancient *piscina*, a stoup for holy water, in the corner, and a 70ft, 14th century tower above me.

There is also a greyhound. A very timid one. It has come with the lady who asks about my route as she jots down a plan for restocking the planters in the churchyard.

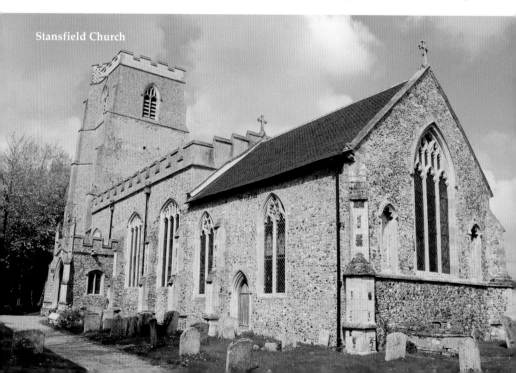
Stansfield Church

There is a splendid display of bright yellow leopard's bane between two graves (**above**), and I compliment her on it. The dog flinches as I reach for my pack and the lady tells me it was a rescue, badly abused, had both hips broken. Poor dog, but it has found a caring home.

The church stands on one hill, the village on another to the south, but my route takes me off to the east, over the fields.

Stansfield to Hawkedon

Footpaths take me out of Stansfield, climbing the rounded fields – the River Glem glinting down to my right – for the hop to Hawkedon in the next valley. The village announces itself via its church, whose tower rises above the trees like so many of the pilgrim points along my route, as I join a quiet lane.

Fifteenth century St Mary's, Hawkedon, stands in splendid isolation, encircled by its stone churchyard wall, and surrounded by the expansive village green. Unlike every other village I have passed through, where the houses cluster in a tight-knit huddle around the church and pub, Hawkedon is spread out. It feels rather like a moorland village in the north.

Its name means 'Hill of the Hawks' in Old English.

In the churchyard the grave of the sadly appropriately named John Alexander Stiff bears the inscription: 'I'd rather be fishing'.

I walk in through the time- and weather-worn south porch at St Mary's,

Below: Approaching Hawkedon across the fields

the saint's niche in the frieze empty, and find a grand church full of unvarnished oak: moulded ceiling, a great supporting beam, and pews all adding the sense of organic growth over centuries.

On the southern fringe of the green is Hawkedon Hall, a lovely 17th and 18th century timber-frame and plaster house painted dusky pink. In its garden are the surviving base and shaft of a 14th or 15th

PILGRIM GHOSTS IN ST MARY'S, HAWKEDON

Splinters of the shattered English pilgrim tradition survive in St Mary's. Above the east window, a dark panel, the remnant of a wall painting, features a scene of the Transfiguration, when Jesus took the disciples Peter, James and John up a mountain, and his face and clothes became dazzlingly bright.

The image is almost invisible today, but a sketch made when it was discovered in 1855 shows St James in his pilgrim hat. And in the window beneath it there is a pilgrim scallop shell. The same window (**left, top**) contains fragments of glass probably smashed during the reign of Henry VIII's son, Edward VI, and later pieced together again.

The poppy-head pew end carvings (**left, bottom**) also suffered. On one, three moustachioed men have been defaced, on another a figure defeating two lions has been blinded, on a third a finely-dressed lady's features are wiped away.

The lower panels of the rood screen survive, with traces of the scenes painted on them. One depicts the 4th century martyr St Dorothy, patron saint of florists, with her basket of flowers.

On the other is what may be St James the Great in his pilgrim hat, or perhaps St Roch (or Rocco), to whom prayers were offered in time of plague.

Roch, incidentally, is the patron saint of dogs and dog lovers, and I am reminded of the lady with her rescued greyhound in Stansfield.

century stone cross. It was once used, according to local legend, as the village barter post. Just to the north is a fine old inn, the 15th century Queen's Head, which I pass as I climb out of the village.

Hawkedon to Rede

A green way leads from the top of the hill on the outskirts of Hawkedon. It winds down to a valley where a narrower path leads off to the right. I miss it and have to retrace my steps but am glad I do because of a huge and magnificent tree stump standing in a field on the wrong route. Once corrected, the path takes me below grand Hawkedon House and up to a lane, before on the edge of Rede a footpath leads me left around a farm to a lovely pub, The Plough. Its mellow paint scheme of green and cream makes it blend into the landscape. As it's the last pub directly on today's route I stop for an early lunch.

Afterwards, it is a short walk up a quiet lane, past a red phone box now stuffed with books for exchange, to the church, All Saints. I pass a terrace of three colour-coordinated cottages – in mustard, mulberry and ochre – that line the approach to the churchyard.

All Saints stands at the highest point in Suffolk, at 380ft. It has been a place of unbroken Christian worship since 976, and may have previously been a pagan site.

From the flint tower, gargoyle waterspouts with long lizard tongues spit rainwater well away from the building. I'm used to seeing stone heads, usually of a king and queen, flanking the entrance to a

Right: All Saints Church, Rede

village church, but here those heads are within, on either side of the chancel arch, staring back at the congregation.

I'm taking a look at them when a local, noticing my interest, tells me that the one on the right looks very like the son of the then-rector, who funded the church's restoration in 1870. He was Arthur Julius Hilgrove Turner who died, aged 23, in Bombay. He also appears in a panel in the east window, depicted as Cornelius the centurion kneeling before St Peter.

My guide leads me outside to two more heads on the west gable, one that looks half man, half cat, the other a lion, carved by someone who had never seen a lion.

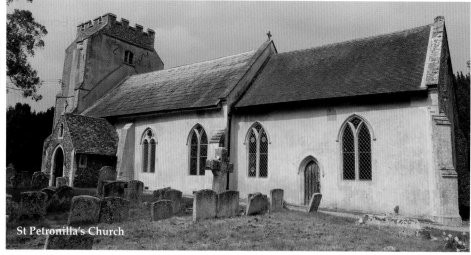

St Petronilla's Church

Rede to Whepstead

I stay in high country from Rede to Whepstead, the rough half-way point and a good spot to split the stage if you plan to tackle it over two days. At first I take to the verges along quiet lanes, but approaching Stone Cross Green an unsigned footpath takes me over the fields to join the Bury to Clare Walk through the fields to the fringes of Whepstead.

Here I add a handsome village sign to my collection, the first I have seen to depict a saint. She is St Petronilla, to whom the church (**above**) is dedicated, and is portrayed pouring water from a jug into the cupped hands of a kneeling woman. The sign stands beside a bus shelter doubling as a book exchange, in which a notice warns: 'Bicycles parked in this bus shelter are left at owners' risk'.

ST PETRONILLA

There is some uncertainly as to who St Petronilla, a 1st century Roman Christian, actually was. She is sometimes referred to as St Peter's daughter, and is often depicted holding a key for him, but she may actually have been a convert of his, and hence a daughter in the spiritual sense.

Whepstead's church was not originally dedicated to Petronilla. It honoured St Thomas, probably of Canterbury, until the 1880s when it was rededicated by those leading the restoration. So why the rededication? Until the Reformation, when Whepstead's church was held by Bury Abbey, income from here helped fund the leper hospital of St Petronilla in the town. In renaming the church, this tradition was being honoured.

Whepstead is a slight diversion from the direct route to Bury, and I had wondered about including it, but I'm glad I did. The church and its saint are intriguing. This is the only church in England dedicated to St Petronilla.

St Petronilla's sits in a tree-shaded churchyard on a rise, a mile east of the main village and next door to Whepstead Hall, suggesting it was built here for the convenience of the squire rather than the congregation.

I perch on a bough of a churchyard yew, which has a handy kink at seat height, and look up at the stump of a tower. It sported a leaded spire until taken in a storm on the night Oliver Cromwell died, 3 September 1658.

This is a homely and welcoming place. Beside the porch entrance, a row of painted stones spell out Alleluia!, and just inside there are jars of preserves for sale.

The restoration here lasted from the 1870s until the 1920s, and is a model of sensitivity. The chancel arch is new, the original having collapsed during restoration, but is decorated with a Norman zigzag pattern. The window arch to the right of it is pierced by the original steps that once led up to the medieval rood loft. They burrow into the wall in such an intriguing way that I'd love to be able to follow them.

St Petronilla's, Whepstead
Top: Chancel arch.
Above: Steps that once led up to the rood loft.

Whepstead to Bury St Edmunds

Leaving the church, I retrace my steps to re-join the Bury to Clare Walk, first on lanes so quiet I see not a single car, through Pinford End and then off over the fields once more. There are no more villages before Bury, making this half of the stage a solitary, contemplative one, which leaves plenty of time for anticipation to build.

As I join the St Edmund Way I look out for my first glimpse of the towers and spires of Bury St Edmunds, but find it doesn't announce itself like Saffron Walden, and so many Suffolk villages. Bury holds the pilgrim in suspense. Not until I am crossing Holywater Meadows, deep in its suburbs, do I spot the tower of St Edmundsbury Cathedral. The sight puts a spring in my step as I walk on through parkland and recreation areas, over the ring road and then up Friars Lane, where the school children are just being passed from teacher to parent, cars clogging the narrow lane.

Then it is past the Greene King Brewery, spreading its sourmash smell over the town, and down Brideswell Lane and Crown St to St Edmundsbury Cathedral.

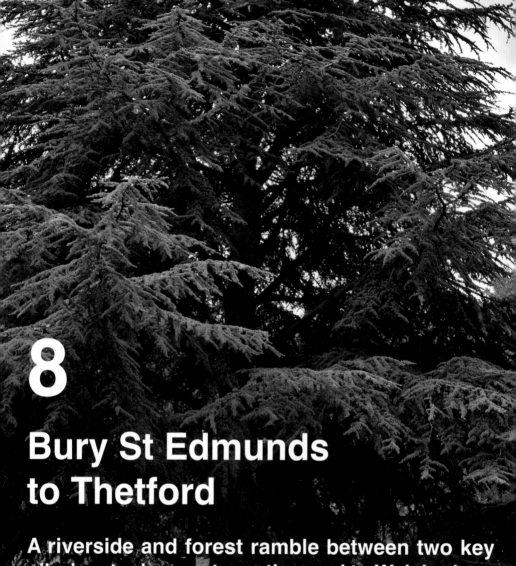

8

Bury St Edmunds to Thetford

A riverside and forest ramble between two key pilgrim staging posts on the road to Walsingham

At the heart of Bury St Edmunds I am enfolded by a holy town. A place that venerates St Edmund, a 10th century king who – before George – was patron saint of England. A town whose cathedral was dedicated to St James the Great of Compostela, patron saint of pilgrims, by an abbot unable to journey to Santiago. Such was the abiding power and legacy of St Edmund that, in the Middle Ages, Bury St

Edmunds was itself one of the most important pilgrim destinations in England. But for many of those pilgrims it was also a key staging post on the Walsingham Way.

The ruins of the abbey church stand on a 14-acre riverside site that is now a wonderfully peaceful park: the green heart of this pilgrim town, and a perfect place for exploration and reflection.

On this stage of the walk I explore this holy ground before setting off to reach the River Lark, following it upriver to Culford, through forest to Barnham and then over the common to a second holy town:

St Edmundsbury Cathedral

Thetford. The walk proves quite a contrast to the bustle of Bury. It passes through a region that is remote, austere: a land for meditation. There is just one village, no pubs or shops, but that is fine, because it takes all this quiet stretch for me to absorb everything I have felt and experienced in Bury.

PRACTICAL INFORMATION

ROUTE OVERVIEW   16.3 miles (26.3km)

Stock up with provisions before you leave Bury St Edmunds today as there are no shops or pubs on this stage and only one place to stay at the halfway mark.

From Bury St Edmunds the route heads out through the suburbs, following the St Edmund Way long distance path alongside the River Lark and then cross country to Culford, reached in **5.6 miles**. From here, leaving the S t Edmund Way, a short stretch along a pavemented B road takes you to Brockley Corner (**1.1 miles**), after which the route follows byways and green ways.

In another **4.3 miles** there is an opportunity to split the stage by turning right along the Icknield Way for a B&B at New Zealand Cottages. If you continue, it is a further **1.9 miles** to the village of Barnham, after which a **1.5 mile** stretch along the A134, on pavements most of the way, then a grass verge, takes you to Barnham Cross Common. The final stretch takes you over Barnham Cross Common and then along the River Little Ouse to reach Thetford in a further **1.9 miles**.

Public transport options

Public transport options are better for this stage, with **train** stations in both Bury St Edmunds and Thetford. Although there are several **bus** services to and from both these towns, the only ones that call at midway points on the stage are the No 84/86, which stops in Barnham, and the infrequent No 332 via Culford. See also public transport map and table pp29-31.

For a **taxi** try Bury St Edmunds-based *A1 Cars* (☎ 01284-766777, 🖳 a1cars.co.uk) or

---

- **Terrain** Mainly riverside and sandy forest tracks over almost entirely flat country
- **Difficulty** Moderate
- **Cumulative distance from London** 116 miles (187km)
- **Time** 5hrs 30mins actual walking time
- **Total ascent** 133.4m, 437ft
- **Maps** OS Explorer *211 Bury St Edmunds & Stowmarket, 229 Thetford Forest*
- **GPX route file & directions*** 508.pdf, 508.gpx, 508.kml at 🖳 https://trailblazer-guides.com/press * See pp27-8 for more information on downloads

there's *A2B Taxis* (☎ 01842-755222, 🖳 www.a2btaxisthetford.co.uk) or *Perry's Taxis* (☎ 07985-386059, 01842-769686, 🖳 perrystaxis.co.uk), both based in Thetford.

Where to eat or stay along the way

● **Bury St Edmunds** (see Stage 7, p109)

● **Near Barnham** (after 10.6 miles/17km) *The Mill B&B* (☎ 01842-890212, 🖳 themillbandb.com, New Zealand Cottages, Barnham). This B&B has four en-suite rooms and is conveniently located 800yds off the route if you would like an overnight stay within the stage. Alternatively, taxis (see above) could be ordered to collect you from Culford or Barnham.

● **Thetford Stay** at *The Bell Hotel*, (☎ 01842-754455, 🖳 greenekinginns.co.uk/hotels/the-bell-hotel-thetford, King St; bars open daily 7am-11pm, **food** daily 7am-9pm) an old coaching inn at the centre of this ancient market town; or reliable chain hotel *Travelodge* (🖳 travelodge.co.uk; Bridge St) located on river, right by the junction of Stages 8 and 9. **Food** options include *Central Café & Restaurant* (☎ 01842-760101; daily 8am-5pm; 1 Whitehart St) which is very popular with locals; and *Tall Orders* (☎ 01842 766435, 🖳 facebook.com/TallOrders-Thetford; Mon-Sat 8.30am-4.30pm, Sun closed) at; 24 King St, which offers coffee, cakes, breakfast and light meals.

Services

● **Bury St Edmunds** (see Stage 7, p109)

● **Thetford** Stock up at **supermarket** Tesco Express (daily 6am-11pm) on Norwich Rd or Aldi (Mon-Sat 8am-10pm, Sun 10am-4pm) on Lime Kiln Ln). If you need a **laundrette** there's aptly named The Laundrette (☎ 07779-136495; daily 7am-9pm) at 39 Icknield Way).

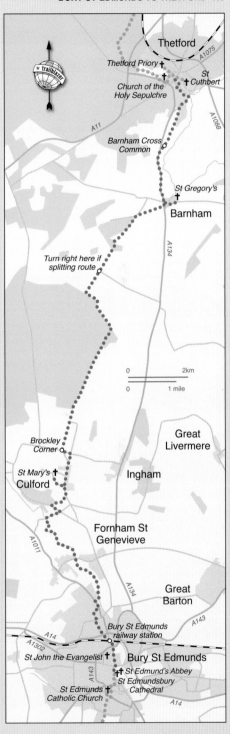

Thetford
Thetford Priory ✝
St Cuthbert ✝
Church of the Holy Sepulchre ✝
A11
A1075
A1088
Barnham Cross Common
St Gregory's ✝
Barnham
A134
Turn right here if splitting route
0   2km
0   1 mile
Brockley Corner
Great Livermere
St Mary's ✝
Culford
Ingham
Fornham St Genevieve
A1011
Great Barton
A134
Bury St Edmunds railway station
A143
A14
A1302
St John the Evangelist ✝
Bury St Edmunds
A143
St Edmund's Abbey ✝
St Edmundsbury Cathedral
St Edmunds ✝ Catholic Church
A14

PILGRIMAGE HIGHLIGHTS

● **Bury St Edmunds** Pilgrim visitors see ⌨ stedscathedral.org/visit/pilgrimage
St Edmund's Abbey (☎ 01284-757490, ⌨ english-heritage.org.uk, Angel Hill; open summer 9am-5pm, winter to 4pm. Ruins of the original abbey, in a riverside park.
St Edmundsbury Cathedral (⌨ stedscathedral.org; open Mon-Fri 10.30am-5pm, Sat 10am-4pm, Sun 12.30-3pm, numerous services, see ⌨ stedscathedral.org/worship for details) **Pilgrim stamp in Cathedral shop, opposite cathedral entrance.**
St Edmund's Catholic church (⌨ stedmundkm.org.uk, 21 Westgate St; open at Mass times, Mon 12.30pm, Tue 9.30am, Wed 10am, Thur 7.30pm, Fri 9.30am, Sat 10am & 6pm, Sun 8.30am & 10.30pm). The original church, dating from penal times when Catholic worship was illegal, is tucked behind the presbytery.
St John the Evangelist (☎ 01284-752906, ⌨ achurchnearyou.com/church/2205, St John's St; open daily 9am-5.30pm, services Wed 9.30am, Sun 11am) The church contains a small statue of Our Lady of Walsingham, and holds a monthly service for the Anglican shrine at Walsingham.
● **Culford** *St Mary* (☎ 01284 753 984, ⌨ achurchnearyou.com/church/2212; open 10am-4pm, services, see website. In the grounds of Culford School, but the postal address is The Street IP32 6JZ). **Pilgrim stamp in church.**
● **Barnham** *St Gregory* (☎ 07546-491388, 01842-890409, ⌨ achurchnearyou.com /church/2141, 4 Euston Rd; open daily, check with church for hours, services 1st Sun 8am, 3rd Sun 10am).

For pilgrimage highlights in Thetford, see Stage 9, p133

Above: Abbey Gate, Bury St Edmunds

Bury St Edmunds

I splash out in Bury St Edmunds, making the four-star *Angel Hotel* my pilgrim hostelry. Well, it's not every day you are half way to Walsingham. In fact I stay two nights, in order to savour all that Bury has to offer the pilgrim. The bill is worth it for the view alone. This morning, from my room on the second floor, I have a perfect panorama before me: the cathedral to my right and the grand 14th century Abbey Gate to my left.

I am by no means the first pilgrim to rest my weary feet at The Angel. It was re-built in the 18th century as a coaching inn, but the surviving 13th century undercroft – and its name – are evidence that for at least seven centuries this was a hostelry for

8

Above: Painted ceiling in the Millennium Tower, St Edmundsbury Cathedral.

pilgrims and others. Indeed, pilgrims have been coming to Bury's abbey for a thousand years, and millennial celebrations take place throughout 2022, having been delayed two years by Covid.

Until the Reformation, pilgrims will have entered through the 12th century Norman Tower, and I walk there from The Angel. It was known in medieval times as the Church Gate, was built as a campanile or bell tower, and is now the cathedral's belfry.

Above: The Angel Hotel has been welcoming pilgrims for centuries

Here, pilgrims will have reported to the porter before being allowed through the arched gateway. Today the tower stands in grand isolation behind iron railings, the pathway several feet below the present ground level.

Medieval pilgrims would have walked on to the abbey church, and the shrine of St Edmund, but neither survived the Reformation, so I go first to the cathedral, alongside the tower. It was built as a church in the 12th century, by Abbot Anselm, only becoming a cathedral in 1914.

When Anselm was unable to go on pilgrimage to Santiago de Compostela, he honoured St James the Great in another way: by building this church within the abbey precincts and dedicating it to the patron saint of pilgrims. Its modern dedication as the Cathedral Church of St James and St Edmund neatly honours both the

THE MYSTERY OF ST EDMUND

St Edmund was one of England's three original patron saints until Edward III replaced him with the more warlike George in 1350. Yet, despite being the subject of a vibrant, dynamic and hugely popular cult, Edmund is something of a mystery figure. Indeed, one of the greatest mysteries surrounding him is what happened to his body, which had disappeared from his shrine by the time the abbey was suppressed in 1539.

This king of East Anglia was martyred in 870 by pagan Danish invaders for refusing to renounce his faith. He was tied to a tree, turned into a pincushion by archers, and then decapitated. Where his martyrdom occurred is not known, but in 903 his body was brought to Bury. Just over a thousand years ago, in 1020, King Canute built a shrine for him in the town. When, in 1095, the great abbey church was built, St Edmund's relics were moved to a bejewelled, gold- and silver-embellished shrine within it.

By the cathedral is a bronze statue of St Edmund by Elisabeth Frink.

The monarchy in particular revered him. A string of kings felt they had a deeply personal relationship with the saint. In 1132, Henry I made a pilgrimage to his shrine, to fulfil a vow made during a storm at sea in which he feared for his life.

In the 13th century, Henry III sent an account of the birth of his second son to the then abbot, in which he wrote: 'When our beloved Consort Eleanor, our queen, was labouring in the pains of childbirth, we had the antiphon of Edmund chanted for her, and when the aforesaid prayer was not yet finished [she had] borne us a son... Know that... as you requested, we are having our son named Edmund'.

In the 14th century, Richard II had a triptych painted in which Edmund, together with Edward the Confessor and John the Baptist, is portrayed presenting him to the Virgin and Christ Child.

The last point in history at which it is known Edmund's body was in the shrine was 1198, when it was opened after being damaged by fire. Some time between then and 1539 it was removed, perhaps by the monks when they realised the abbey was bound to fall to Henry VIII's desecrators. There is a theory that Edmund's remains were placed in an iron chest and reburied somewhere in the abbey grounds.

Left: Ceiling and organ above the quire, St Edmundsbury Cathedral.

pilgrim saint and the saintly king, and places pilgrimage at the heart of veneration here.

I step inside. This is a simple space, clean and cool, but with some spectacular modern painted ceilings. They are so splendid that I wish I could lie on my back on a trolley and be towed around beneath them. The Millennium Tower, with the loveliest, jewel-like ceiling, was completed only in 2005, powerful evidence that this is a place where faith and veneration are still very much alive.

From the cathedral I walk through the Pilgrim Herb Garden, planted with medicinal plants used by medieval monks, and into a circular park filled on a bright spring day with people out to catch the early sun. The grounds run down to the River Lark, which will later guide me onwards.

Above: Sculpture in the Pilgrim Herb Garden.

There are many treasures in the expansive abbey grounds. Among them are Elisabeth Frink's statue of St Edmund and, my quirky favourite, the houses that have been built in the ruined walls of monastery buildings. Their grand stone windows and stout doors peer out through the rubble walls they occupy, reminding me of hermit crabs squatting in the discarded shells of others.

The focus for medieval pilgrims would have been Edmund's shrine in the abbey church, and I walk there next. Today, that building survives as just a series of abstract shapes, the vaguest ghost of a church, but look through those ruins to where Anselm's church, now the cathedral, rises with its modern tower, and Bury's past, present and future-promise all come into focus.

There are two other pilgrim points in Bury, and I visit them during an amble around the town. One is the Catholic church of St Edmund, which offers a stately, classical porticoed frontage to Westgate St, but hides the original secret chapel behind its presbytery. The chapel was established in 1760, in a time when

Left: Pilgrims would have entered the abbey through the 12th-century Church Gate, now the cathedral's belfy.

8

Above: Post-Reformation, houses were crafted from the ruins of the monastery.

Above: A monthly Holy House Mass is celebrated at the Church of St John the Evangelist.

Catholicism was illegal, and only officially licensed for Catholic worship in 1791.

The second is Anglican St John the Evangelist in St John's St, a striking early-Victorian Gothic creation, in brick, with a 170ft landmark spire, in which 60 nesting boxes for swifts have been incorporated.

This is something of an outpost for Walsingham, with a monthly Mass offered for the Holy House at the Anglican shrine. A diminutive statue of Our Lady of Walsingham perches on a ledge beside a pillar in the nave.

Below: Ruins of the original abbey church in Abbey Gardens, Bury St Edmunds.

Bury to Culford

The morning after my day of comparative rest, I walk up Angel Hill to Northgate St, my head buzzing with the wonders of Bury and the story of St Edmund. I span the thundering A14 via a footbridge, pass through a brief band of suburbia, and am out in the countryside. The St Edmund Way takes me to the River Lark, which I encountered yesterday in the abbey gardens, and which will be my faithful guide for the first stage of my way to Thetford.

To my left is a golf course, to my right, beyond the deep-flowing river, I can just make out the tower of the ruined church of St Genevieve above the trees. It was destroyed in 1775, it is said, when a man shooting jackdaws from the tower managed to set it alight.

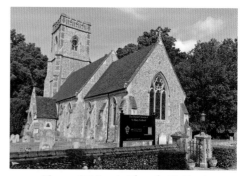

Above: St Mary's Church, Culford

At the splendidly named Ducksluice Farm, where the path switches banks, I hear the persistent call of a cuckoo, brazen con merchant. I leave the Lark and let the St Edmund Way guide me to Culford, where, after a brief roadside stretch, I enter Culford Park, its 480 acres landscaped by Humphrey Repton in the 18th century to complement Culford Hall, now a school. Once, all this belonged to the abbey at Bury St Edmunds. After the Reformation it fell, over the centuries, into the hands of a string of wealthy families, including the Benyons and, in 1889, the 5th Earl Cadogan.

Alongside the house is a church, St Mary's, standing beneath stately pines on an immaculately clipped green carpet. This is a Victorian building with a Norman heart, and many 14th century features. St Mary's was rebuilt in 1856, at great expense, by Edward Richard Benyon who, as well as owning Culford Hall, was an Anglican priest, and rector of the church he re-created. He had it built around an extraordinary memorial, dating from 1656, to Lady Jane Bacon, wife of Nathaniel, an artist, who has his own memorial beneath the tower.

Jane's memorial is a remarkably touching testament to motherhood, and loss. She sits, in white marble, with her baby grand-

Below: Culford Park

Above: Memorial to Lady Jane Bacon, St Mary's Church, Culford

Above and below: On the trail between Culford and Barnham

daughter on her lap, in an echo of representations of Mary and Jesus. She is surrounded by a daughter and several great grand-children, all of whom died in infancy. Lying at her feet is her adult son, Nicholas, who died childless aged 43.

Culford to Barnham

That monument gives me further food for thought as I walk back to the village and on along the pavement for the short stretch to Brockley Corner. Here, I exchange tarmac for a sandy, green way that passes the Hill of Health, site of a Bronze Age bowl-shaped burial mound.

The green way runs on, die-straight, with a wide-open landscape of fields to my right and a forest to my left. Its patchwork of names – Deal Furze, Griffin's Covert, Jerry's Old Plantation – belies its monolithic appearance. A belt of silver birch flanks the path, the forest floor green underfoot, softening the edge of the deep, dark wood beyond, where the pines shut out the light.

The sand muffles my footsteps and the strong wind in my face – straight from Siberia – takes my scent away, leading to regular encounters with wildlife. A grey-brown creature that is either a very small muntjac or a very large hare comes lolloping into view. Finally aware of me, it pulls up short, flicks its ears and is off. It's a hare.

Then comes a plunge through the woods on the approach to Culford Heath. I duck under a barrier blocking the track to 4x4s that might otherwise pioneer their way along these old droving roads, the sand giving way to an equally soft blanket

of pine needles. At the far side of the forest is another historic encounter: for a short stretch I join the Icknield Way Trail, a modern interpretation of a route that may date to prehistoric times. This is a lonely, largely unoccupied stretch. A rare cottage – a thatch, flint and weatherboard place in the cheerily named Happi Holme – is tucked behind a hedge tall and thick enough to take the edge off those Siberian blasts.

From here the landscape opens out beneath a great, blue bell-jar sky. With the forest behind me, I cross a patchwork of fields that mix blocks of bright spring green and

Below: Church of St Gregory, Barnham

oilseed-rape yellow with the occasional square shimmering under polythene. A skylark lifts at my feet, a blur of yellow-brown spiralling up as its song spills out like a jazz solo.

Here you see the power of the wind: a straggle of firs that line the path have been buffeted and misshaped as they struggle to grow against it. In places a bough as thick as a telegraph pole has been snapped off as if it were a twig. The tracks are as sandy as a beach and, as I shuffle through the drifts, I remember the feel of silky sand between my toes.

To my left is a great field full of pigs (**right**). Beside the track it is restaurant

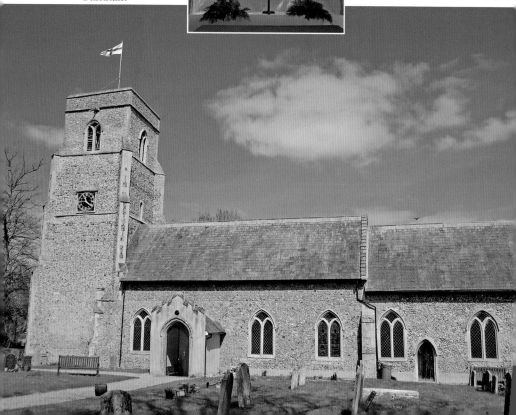

row, troughs lined up like a series of fast food joints. At one of them, pigs-behaving-badly are in the trough along with the food. In more swine-friendly weather, they might be wallowing in mud, as it is they throw up dust trails as they trot along, like cowboys galloping over the prairie. Across the way a tractor sets up an even bigger dust storm. I read somewhere that, before the coniferous forests were put down in the last century, this border territory spanning Suffolk and Norfolk was a dustbowl. So the forest is here to pin the land in place.

When I am 10.8 miles into the walk I reach a point where, if I were splitting this stage into two, I could turn right and follow the Icknield Way for 800 yards to reach The Mill B&B. But I forge on, leaving forest and expansive fields for grassy sheep country, crossing the disused line of the Bury to Thetford railway through a gap in an old embankment. Traffic lights take me safely over the A134 and down the lane to Barnham.

Alongside the church of St Gregory, Barnham offers the pilgrim a bench on a green sprinkled with daisies and buttercups. Here I eat lunch. It is close to April 23, and the flag of St George flutters from the top of the tower.

Hunger handled, I enter this simple country church, with its orange and cream chequerboard floor tiles, plain white walls and luminous stained glass. Flowers abound.

On the north wall is a huge collage: a portrait of the village and its people, showing every house and naming each inhabitant, as recorded in the 1911 census. It's a wonderfully loving tribute from today's villagers to those who have gone before them, just as affecting as the very different memorial at Culford. It reminds me that every pilgrim needs a home to return to.

Barnham to Thetford

A mile and a half past Barnham I cross from Suffolk into Norfolk, and reach Barnham Cross Common, where I can leave the verge of the A134 to walk cross-country to the outskirts of Thetford. There, I turn onto Nuns' Bridges Rd, the name recalling a monastery that was an offshoot of the abbey at Bury St Edmunds.

Just before the point at which the Nuns' Bridges span the River Little Ouse and the River Thet was the Priory of St George, a nunnery founded in around 1020, when King Canute was establishing the Benedictines at Bury. The bridges carried the Icknield Way over the waters and the house called the Nunnery is now the headquarters of the British Ornithological Trust.

I take just the first of the bridges, then turn left to follow the River Little Ouse over a string of islands to Thetford, my resting place for the night. As I relax after my arrival, I reflect that a theme I had not anticipated has emerged on this stage of my pilgrimage. It is one of loss and remembrance, and the ways in which grief, that great leveller, has affected saints, kings and people like you and me.

9

Thetford to Brandon

A riverside walk from Thetford Priory, via a holy well and little forest church, to the pilgrim town of Brandon

For medieval pilgrims forging on from Bury St Edmunds towards Walsingham, the next key point of veneration was Thetford. They were drawn here because, at the riverside Priory of Our Lady, stood a statue of the Virgin Mary which was said to perform miracles.

Henry VIII visited – and venerated – this place, which had a particularly personal importance for him. For it contained the tomb of

his illegitimate son, Henry FitzRoy, who died of consumption at the age of 17. Because of that, this was one of the last of the monasteries Henry seized and, when he did, the bones of his dead son had to be taken elsewhere.

There are other key pilgrim places in Thetford, and I explore them before heading west on a wonderful walk alongside the River Little Ouse, via a holy well and one of England's smallest churches, to the next staging post on the medieval Walsingham Way: the town of Brandon, where several pilgrim routes converge.

The ruins of Thetford Priory

PRACTICAL INFORMATION

ROUTE OVERVIEW   10.5 miles (16.9km)

This is a short, easy stage with good services and transport links at the start and end. There is nowhere to eat or stay between the two at Santon Downham, but there are public toilets in the car parks. You would need to use a bus or taxi to divide this section into two shorter ones.

This comparatively short stage begins by taking in the pilgrim highlights of Thetford, then follows the St Edmund Way alongside the River Little Ouse before a short climb to a forest stretch, reaching St Helen's Oratory and Holy Well in **5.4 miles**. There is a descent to cross the Little Ouse, then a walk along forest tracks and a lane via All Saints, to reach St Mary's, Santon Downham in a further **1.9 miles**. The route leaves the St Edmund Way at this point.

From Santon Downham, the path is once again alongside the river, now following the route of the Little Ouse Path, reaching Brandon in **2.9 miles**, then following High St (A1065) to the end of the stage at Brandon's railway station, reached in a further **0.3 miles**.

Public transport options

This stage is well connected by both **train**, with stations at Thetford and Brandon, and **bus**, with services including the No 40 Thetford to Kings Lynn, the No 84/86 Brandon to Bury St Edmunds and the No 200/201 Thetford to Mildenhall, of which four buses a day travel via Santon Downham. See also public transport map and table pp29-31.
There are two car parks in Santon Downham where a car could be left or a taxi pick-up arranged. St Helen's Trail car park (toilets; open summer only, dawn-dusk; IP27 0TJ) just past All Saints church; and at the Forestry Commission Offices (toilets; 9am-4pm; off Mark Ln IP27 0TJ) just before the lane crosses the river Little Ouse.
Taxi firms include *A2B Taxis* (☎ 01842-755222, 🖳 www.a2btaxisthetford.co.uk) or *Perry's Taxis* (☎ 07985-386059, 01842-769686, 🖳 perrystaxis.co.uk), both based in Thetford, and in Brandon there's *Carters Brandon Cars* (☎ 01842-811430, 🖳 cartersbrandoncars.co.uk).

Where to eat or stay along the way

● **Thetford** (see Stage 8, p119)

- ● **Terrain** Riverside and forest paths   ● **Difficulty** Easy
- ● **Cumulative distance from London** 126.5 miles (203.9km)
- ● **Time** 3hrs 40mins actual walking time   ● **Total ascent** 123metres/403ft
- ● **Map** OS Explorer *229 Thetford Forest in the Brecks*
- ● **GPX route file & directions*** 509.pdf, 509.gpx, 509.kml at 🖳 https://trailblazer-guides.com/press * See pp27-8 for more information on downloads

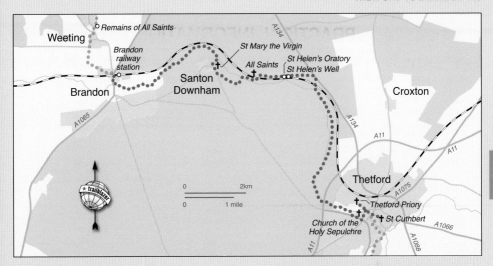

● **Brandon Stay, eat** or **camp** at historic *Ram Inn* (☎ 01842-810275, 🖳 facebook.com then search Ram Inn Brandon; High St; pub open Mon-Thur 11am-11pm, Fri-Sat 11am-1am, Sun noon-11, food: check for Mon-Sat times, Sun noon-3.30). Hotel, bar, restaurant, campsite. Pleasant inn with 16 rooms, which has been hosting pilgrims and travellers since 1349. Alternatively the *Bridge Hotel* (☎ 01842-338228, 🖳 bridgehotelbrandon.com; 79 High St) is a 200-year-old, family-run riverside hotel with seven rooms.

Services
● **Thetford** (see Stage 8, p119)
● **Brandon** On the High St is **supermarket** Aldi (Mon-Sat 8am-10pm, Sun 10am-4pm), while the **laundrette** (☎ 01842-813111; daily 9am-9pm) is at 11 Stores St.

PILGRIMAGE HIGHLIGHTS

● **Thetford** *St Cuthbert'*s (🖳 thetfordteamministry.org.uk; open check website, services Sun & Wed 10.30am, 1 King St). **Pilgrim stamp in church.** On Water Lane, *Thetford Priory* (☎ 0370-3331181, 🖳 english-heritage.org.uk/visit/places/thetford-priory; open 8am-6pm, to 4pm winter) was once the burial place of Henry VIII's illegitimate son. *Church of the Holy Sepulchre* (🖳 english-heritage.org.uk; Brandon Rd) Access restricted during conservation work but can be viewed easily from the gate leading onto the site.
● (after 5.5 miles/8.5km) *St Helen's Oratory and Holy Well* is open at all times.
● **Santon** (after 6.2 miles/10km) *All Saints* (🖳 santondownham.org/about/all-saints, Santon Houses; open daily, no services) redundant church now in the care of Norfolk Churches Trust.

THETFORD PRIORY AND A PLEA TO HENRY VIII

The 12th century Priory of Our Lady of Thetford was one of the largest and most important monasteries in medieval East Anglia, and the burial place of the Earls and Dukes of Norfolk for 400 years.

The body of Henry VIII's son, Henry FitzRoy, Duke of Richmond, came here because he had been married to Norfolk's daughter, Mary Howard, and the king entrusted the funeral arrangements to Norfolk. Richmond's mother was Henry's mistress, Elizabeth Blount, and had been born during Henry's marriage to Catherine of Aragon. He was the only illegitimate son Henry acknowledged and, for a time, the king planned to make him his heir, despite his illegitimacy.

The Duke of Norfolk hoped Richmond's presence in his family tomb at the priory would sway Henry when he petitioned to have this monastery spared. Its suppression was delayed by four years, but in 1540 it went the way of every other monastic house. The Howard family tomb was moved to St Michael's Church, Framlingham, and Richmond's body with it.

Thetford

Thetford is a sleepy market town with a powerful pilgrim past. In the Middle Ages it was dominated by religious houses and had 22 churches. I take a stroll to 13th century St Cuthbert's, one of only three surviving medieval churches. It perches on the corner of Market Place, beside the Guildhall and the Red Lion, at Thetford's historic heart.

Such was Thetford's dependence on the pilgrim trade that, at the time of the Dissolution – when Cluniac, Dominican,

Above: St Cuthbert's Church, Thetford

Augustinian, Benedictine and other monasteries were being dismantled – the town sent a formal complaint to Thomas Cromwell, protesting that so many townsfolk depended on pilgrims for their livelihoods that they faced extreme poverty should those houses fall.

Of course, the appeal fell on deaf ears, and only fragments of Thetford's rich religious past survive. St Cuthbert's is one, a still-vibrant link with that history. It has Saxon roots, an 11th century font probably taken from another church, and a 19th century tower. When I visit, plans are well underway for the creation of a social enterprise café, and Revd Peter Herbert readily accepts the offer of a pilgrim stamp.

I walk east through the pedestrianised town centre to the most prominent pilgrim destination, the ruins of Thetford Priory, beside the River Little Ouse. I am meeting two fellow pilgrims here, and we will walk on to Brandon as a trio, plus dog.

This was a house of the Cluniac Order, great supporters of pilgrims headed for

Above: Pilgrims en route to Walsingham stopped at the now ruined Thetford Priory to venerate holy relics said to include part of Christ's robe, Mary's girdle and even a piece of the manger.

Santiago de Compostela. It takes an effort of imagination to picture the priory as it was, but I do my best as we wander around the ghostly ruins. At first I see just details: a spindle of wall rising from the foundations of the abbey church; a curtain wall from the prior's lodgings, but gradually things come together. I pace out the cloister, and see that, in the chapter house to the east of it, the remains of the monks' bench still line the walls. To the south is the refectory, where the location of a raised pulpit is visible high in the wall, and from which the monks were read to as they ate in silence.

But it's really only when I bring to mind the remarkable story within these stones that the place comes to life for me. Pilgrims travelling from Bury St Edmunds towards Walsingham were drawn here, to this priory dedicated to Our Lady, because of a remarkable legend.

In the 13th century, Mary appeared three times in the dreams of a Thetford artisan suffering from an incurable complaint. She told him he would be restored to health if he could persuade the prior to build a Lady Chapel in stone beside his church. The prior began to build, but only in wood.

Then came a remarkable discovery: a long-forgotten wooden statue of the Virgin. It was found that a hollow carved into its head contained some remarkable relics, with identifying descriptions engraved on lead wrappings. Among them were, reputedly, a relic from Jesus's robe, another from his manger, a third from Mary's girdle, plus the relics of a whole list of saints. A letter with the remains said that they had been sent from the Church of the Holy Sepulchre in Jerusalem at the request of Hugh Bigod, who founded the priory in 1103. A series of miraculous cures followed the discovery, and the pilgrims' offerings enabled the abbot to revise his building plans, creating a Lady Chapel in stone.

There is one further pilgrim location I want to show my fellow pilgrims before we leave Thetford: the remains of a Thetford namesake of the Church of the Holy

Above: Ruins of the Church of the Holy Sepulchre, Thetford

Sepulchre in Jerusalem. It is on the opposite bank of the Little Ouse from the priory, and we take a footbridge across to it.

The original Holy Sepulchre church was built at the point where St Helena – mother of Constantine the Great, the 4th century Roman emperor – discovered the True Cross on which Jesus was crucified while she was on pilgrimage to Jerusalem. St Helena, or Helen, will crop up again during today's walk.

The ruins of Thetford's Holy Sepulchre are the sole surviving remains in England of a priory of the canons of the Holy Sepulchre, who aided medieval pilgrims on their way to Jerusalem. The church became a barn and, in the 19th century, the ruins were adapted as an ornamental garden grotto. Today it sits tucked in among the little houses on a modern estate, an unregarded jewel, but still a place with great resonance if you can see beyond its diminished physical presence. We lean on the gate and give it our best shot.

Thetford to St Helen's Oratory and Holy Well

Back on the riverbank, the St Edmund Way, doubling as the Little Ouse Path, guides us out along my first big river since Ware. The Ouse slides along beside us all the way to Brandon, slowed by weirs, just the odd dimple and swirl to show this is water and that it's on the move. On this, the stillest of days, no wind ruffles the waters. Litter pickers in kayaks are sliding along close to the bank, plucking detritus from overhanging branches. Those trees are about to leaf and are covered in a light haze of green. The water is not so much wine dark as beer-bottle brown, but crystal clear, and fronds of weed sway in the current as if a long-haired swimmer were gliding beneath the surface.

The path forsakes the river for a stretch, passing beneath the railway and up through the forest for a hundred-yard dash alongside the A134. We are able to distance ourselves from the traffic by walking through the trees, before a long, straight forest track draws us back toward the River Little Ouse, where I must keep my eyes open for the remains of an oratory, and a holy well.

Without the interpretation board standing beside the track, I would have had no idea that I was looking at St Helen's Oratory, rather than just a rough mound. Walk to the edge and you see how the railway line has cut into this holy hill. Beyond it is

Left: The path follows the banks of the beer-bottle-brown River Little Ouse.

Above: Picnicing by the site of St Helen's Oratory and Holy Well.

the river and, on the far-side, meadows where a few campers have pitched their tents. Wild swimmers are splashing in the water. We sit and eat our sandwiches, gazing at the view.

This church's dedication is to the same Helen – or Helena – who, as mentioned above, found the True Cross and whose son Constantine built the Church of the Holy Sepulchre. The church, or oratory, here was abandoned in medieval times, and excavation has been undertaken only on a small part of the site, but it uncovered substantial remains of walls and foundations of what was likely a pre-Conquest church. Roman brick had been reused in it, meaning this could be a very early Christian – and possibly pre-Christian – site. Roman pottery was also found, and a grave marker from the 10th or 11th century.

To the left of the grassy hill, beneath which the church is buried, is woodland, and just within the trees is hidden the edge of a deep, flat bottomed bowl cut into the hill. This was a chalk and flint quarry, dug in the 19th century. We wind our way down the steep side in search of the holy well. Often such expeditions end in disappointment: a well turns out to be no more than a damp patch in the leaves. Not here. This is a wide expanse of water, like a river springing fully formed from the earth, into a pool bright with marsh marigolds, the yellow flag irises just waiting to replace them in spring's flower-filled cycle.

The railway crosses just below the well on an embankment, in which the engineers placed a grey-brick arch, so that the flints could be transported by boat out onto the river and away to Thetford or Brandon.

Although the oratory is long gone, the association with St Helen has persisted down the centuries. This is one of at least 25 holy wells dedicated to the saint in eastern England, but the only one in Norfolk.

St Helen's Oratory to Santon Downham
We press on through the woods, high above the river for a stretch, before passing over it on a footbridge where, on the edge of Thetford Forest and beside Santon House, we find All Saints, one of England's smallest, most charming churches. In a connection with the well just visited, it is known by some as St Helen's.

Once there was a village here, and a moated farmhouse, today just three houses and the church, long redundant but still much visited. I get a sudden vision of a gingerbread house. If it weren't for its little crenellated octagonal tower peeking above the roofline, I would feel like I was walking up the garden path to a cottage as I open and carefully close the gate to the lit-

Above: All Saints, Santon, one of the smallest churches in England

tle graveyard, where a man with a strimmer is hard at work.

All Saints has seen some ups and downs: abandoned at the Reformation, remodelled in the 17th century, and again in the 19th. It's the sweetest little church: the nave roof a galaxy of gold stars on blue, in panels separated by red beams painted with flowers; a diminutive roodscreen before a dolls-house chancel; and a miniature reredos tiled like a Victorian fireplace.

Now, down in the river valley, we take a forest track to Santon Downham, and another church. St Mary the Virgin calls itself 'the church in the forest' but it doesn't have the romance of All Saints. And it's locked. From here it is downhill again, through the village. We pass a house with windows like wide-open eyes and two tall, slim chimneys reminding me of arms raised in a stick 'em up gesture, and over a white lattice-work bridge. Here the path rejoins the river, and shadows it all the way to Brandon.

Above: St Mary the Virgin, Santon Downham

Santon Downham to Brandon

There is a touch of the primeval about the path here. It winds on the riverbank through woods where half the trees are dead men standing. One has toppled into the waters of the Little Ouse and is up-ended, its boughs stuck in the mud, its roots waving in the air. I think of a disembodied hand, scampering.

The Little Ouse Path delivers us to Brandon, the next key staging post on the medieval pilgrim route to Walsingham. Today it is a busy thoroughfare, often clogged with traffic, the main road lined with a string of hotels that carry the dust of all those vehicles. Martin D. Locker, in his thesis, *Landscapes of Pilgrimage in Medieval Britain*, points out that Brandon was on a pilgrim crossroads: with routes converging here from Bury St Edmunds, Thetford and Ely. Here, pilgrims headed for Walsingham would converge, crossing the River Little Ouse on their way to the Holy House. There was also a small chapel of St Mary on the bridge.

Erasmus – the 16th century Dutch philosopher, scholar and Catholic priest who went on frequent pilgrimages – passed through Brandon on his way to

Left: Walking through the woods, high above the River Little Ouse

Walsingham from Cambridge. In his colloquies (journals) on pilgrimage he places Brandon among the key towns for overnight stops. The Bishop of Ely owned the bridge, and his personal bailiff was on hand to collect the tolls for using it. Cathedral records from the 15th century show that a hermit called John Herryman was given the job of keeping the bridge, and a small hermitage beside it, in good repair.

The path from Thetford brings us into Brandon by that bridge, which hides its history under a film of anonymising dust. I'm staying in the **Bridge Hotel** alongside it. That hostelry was not around in pilgrim days, but the **Ram Inn** alongside it was, and I bid farewell to my fellow pilgrims over a beer in its garden. The Ram dates from 1349 and will have sheltered pilgrims alongside general travellers. Today it offers a campsite – a real rarity on the London to Walsingham Camino route – alongside beds under its roof.

Just to the north is Brandon's railway station, where this stage ends, and I walk my companions to it before turning in.

Below: Following the river from Santon Downham to Bandon

10

Brandon to
Great Cressingham

Discovering a surviving stretch
of the Walsingham Way, and a
string of medieval pilgrim places

This is a land of ghosts. The ghosts of pilgrims past, who
walked the Walsingham Way from the Augustinian house at
Brandon, guided by a great cross on a hill beyond Weeting, its
now-severed shaft hidden in the forest; and on via a pilgrim
hostelry at Ickburgh and a wayside chapel at Hilborough.

Much of that history is elusive, so I must be something of a pilgrim archaeologist and ghost hunter on this stage of the Walsingham Camino. And while these mementoes may not be the most tangible reminders of medieval pilgrimage, they are still profoundly moving and inspiring. And, like a water diviner whose dowsing rod is beginning to twitch, I can feel a physical sense of Walsingham coming closer as I enter the final quarter of my journey.

St Mary's Church, Weeting

PRACTICAL INFORMATION

ROUTE OVERVIEW   15.6 miles (25.1km)

This stage is well supplied with pubs and neatly divides in half at Mundford which has good facilities to stay and eat plus a shop for provisions, but very little in the way of bus services – taxis are the best way to leave or rejoin the route.

The first half of this stage, starting from Brandon railway station, is almost completely flat. It is a **1.7 mile** walk, mainly via farm tracks to Weeting, and St Mary's church and Weeting Castle. A further **2 miles** on forest tracks takes you to the Stump Cross, the remains of a huge medieval pilgrim waymarker. It is a further **3.2 miles** in forest to Mundford, where the Crown Hotel offers an ideal lunch point, or overnight stay if you are splitting this stage into two.

The second half of the stage is again mainly on the level, initially alongside the A1065, on pavement, verge and forest margin, for **1.9 miles** until you reach the Desert Rats Memorial. From here the route runs through woodland, followed by a short section on the verge of the A1065, before a brief, steady climb on a footpath to All Saints', Hilborough, reached in a further **4.9 miles**. The final stretch is again along pavement beside the A1065, then a short walk on the verge, followed by quiet lanes and a gentle climb to Great Cressingham, reached in another **1.9 miles.**

Public transport options

Brandon, at the beginning of this stage, has both a **train** station and **bus** services (No 84/86 from Bury St Edmunds and No 200/201 from Thetford) but from there you're heading deep into the countryside again. The only bus service along the route is the No 40 which calls infrequently in Mundford. See also public transport map and table pp29-31.

Taxis are the best option. Among local firms are *Carters Brandon Cars* (☎ 01842-811430, ⌨ cartersbrandoncars.co.uk).

Where to eat or stay along the way

● **Brandon** (see Stage 9, p133)
● **Mundford** (after 7.3 miles/11.7km) The welcoming *Crown Hotel and Restaurant* (☎ 01842-878233, ⌨ the-crown-hotel.co.uk, Crown Rd; open Mon-Sat 11am-11pm, Sun noon-10.30pm, food daily noon-3pm, 6.30pm-9pm) serves good **pub grub** and has 40 en-suite **rooms**.

● **Terrain** Mainly forest tracks and quiet lanes over almost completely flat land
● **Difficulty** Moderate
● **Cumulative distance from London** 142.1 miles (229km)
● **Time** 5hrs 10mins actual walking time   ● **Total ascent** 141metres (462ft)
● **Maps** OS Explorer 229 *Thetford Forest, 236 King's Lynn, Downham Mkt & Swaffham*
● **GPX route file & directions*** 510.pdf, 510.gpx, 510.kml at ⌨ https://trailblazer-guides.com/press * See pp27-8 for more information on downloads

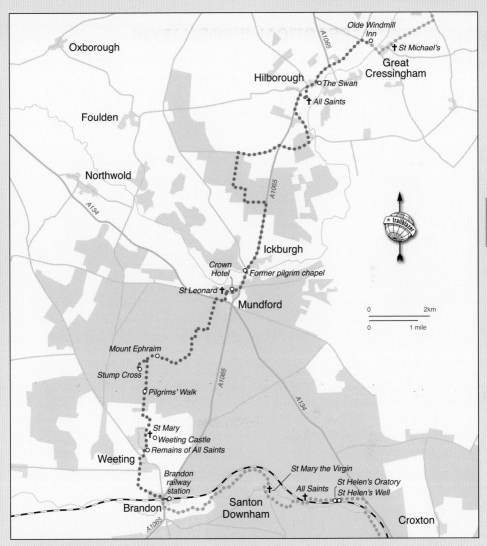

● **Hilborough** (after 13.8 miles / 22.2km) *The Swan Inn* (☎ 01760-756380, 🖥 facebook
.com / hilboroughswan, Brandon Rd; open Mon-Sat 11.30am-11pm, Sun 11am-11pm, food
Mon-Sat 9am-9pm, Sun noon-8pm;), a pleasant village inn with eight en-suite rooms.
● **Great Cressingham** With 15 en-suite **rooms** and hearty **pub grub**, the 17th century
Olde Windmill Inn (☎ 01760-756232, 🖥 oldewindmillinn.co.uk, Water End; daily noon-
10pm, food daily noon-2.30pm & 5.30-9pm) has been run by the same family for 55 years.
It also has a Caravan Club **campsite**.

Services
● **Mundford** Invaluable **convenience store** Yallops Mundford & Post Office (☎ 01842-
878287, St Leonards St; Mon-Sat 6am-8.30pm, Sun 8am-5pm), on the village green.

PILGRIMAGE HIGHLIGHTS

- **Weeting** *St Mary the Virgin* (☎ 01842-827152, 🖳 achurchnearyou.com/church/13973, Home Farm Lane; open for services, see link on website;)
- **Weeting Castle** (🖳 english-heritage.org.uk/visit/places/weeting-castle, Castle Cl; open: daily 9am-5pm). More a point of general historic interest.
- **North of Weeting** *Stump Cross* (see GPX or KML files for exact location, or navigate on Ordnance Survey Explorer map to E577287 N291422)
- **Mundford** *St Leonard* (☎ 01366-328921, 🖳 achurchnearyou.com/church/4737, Church Ln; open for services Sun 10am)
- **Ickburgh** *Our Lady and St Lawrence* (2 Folden Rd) Former pilgrim chapel and hostelry, now Bridge House, and private, but visible from the road.
- **Hilborough** *All Saints* (🖳 achurchnearyou.com/church/10240, off A1065; see website for open hours and service times).

For pilgrimage highlights in Great Cressingham see Stage 11, p156

Brandon to Weeting

Once, Bromehill Priory stood just to the north of Brandon's railway station. There are railway sidings at this spot today, where great dusty pyramids of sand and gravel brought in by train are transferred to trucks and taken onward.

I stand with three fellow pilgrims on the footbridge over the rail lines and survey the scene.

No amount of imagination can conjure up a vision of what was once a key staging post on the road to Walsingham. The priory belonged to the Augustinian canons, the same order as at the priory in Walsingham, and was dedicated to Our Lady and St Thomas of Canterbury.

No trace remains now, and the Walsingham Way – which once led past the priory and on to Weeting – is overlaid for a

THE PILGRIM HOSTELRY AT BROMEHILL PRIORY

The Augustinians were vital guides for Walsingham pilgrims. As Leonard Whatmore notes in *Highway to Walsingham*: 'Their houses in Norfolk nearly all seem to lie on routes that would be frequented by pilgrims to Walsingham, at least a dozen of them.'

Whatmore adds that the welcome at Bromehill, founded in the early 13th century, may not have been a warm one: 'The rule of charitable hospitality would have meant pilgrims were welcomed here but not, apparently, with open arms... the premises were rather shabby, and there were complaints from visiting nobility about the quality of food, beds and lamps.'

When Francis Blomefield wrote his *History of Norfolk* in 1739 he reported that the walls and foundations of the priory could still be seen, and that 'several stone coffins have been dug up.'

10

while by the busy Brandon Rd, but a parallel route along farm tracks will take us onward.

Medieval pilgrims often had to rely on stone crosses to guide them on their way to Walsingham, and travellers looking to the northern horizon from here would have been able to see one. It was on a hill way to the north of the village of Weeting.

Smashed at the Reformation or later, and the area covered in forest in the last century, it is no longer visible from here, but its stump still exists, and my Ordnance Survey map shows me a path called Pilgrim's Walk leading towards its location. But first we have to get there.

Gingerly, we cross the A1065 at a blind bend that drivers treat as a test of tyres

and nerve and are able to pick up a track that peels off Brandon Rd and takes us to

the village of Weeting. It's a relief to leave traffic-blighted Brandon behind, and my expectations are high as we pass The Row, a charming terrace of white-painted thatched cottages (**above**) beside Weeting's village green.

On the green is a village sign with, tucked away on one ceramic face of the supporting plinth: two pilgrims, a man in a cowled cloak leading a horse on which a woman sits. This is the first reference I've seen to the tradition of pilgrimage to Walsingham on the many miles I have walked so far, and it raises my spirits. We are now walking the ancient Walsingham Way. The closer I get to my destination, the stronger the echoes of the pilgrim past become.

Pilgrims will have found two churches on their way through Weeting, today only one remains. We pass the site of the first, All Saints,

Above: St Mary's, Weeting

tucked in a playing field behind a row of bungalows. It survives only as a bulge in the lawn that blankets the foundations. Gravestones are stacked along a fence. We reach the second church shortly after the lane that runs along the fringe of the modern village becomes a dusty farm track.

St Mary's has a round tower: only the second I have seen on my journey from London, and the first in Norfolk. It stands beside the moated ruins of Weeting Castle – actually a 12th century manor house – and may have started life as the manorial chapel attached to it. We pause to look around, and learn that, not only was this not a castle, it wasn't even fortified: the moat added simply to demonstrate the wealth and power of its owner. The walk back from it gives a lovely view of St Mary's over a meadow.

Cawing crows are wheeling from their nests in the treetops around the church yard, and a pair of bushy yews guard its door like a particularly fine set of sideburns. It makes a curiously sinister entrance to a church, I can't help thinking. The porch doors are chained, it has no name board, sign or note about keyholders, and looks abandoned, yet I see through the windows that there are fresh flowers in vases on the window sills.

On a later visit, by chance I meet a lady waiting for a fire extinguisher engineer who lets me in, and find the flowers are actually plastic but very realistic. The pews to one side of the aisle are cordoned off because some patches of plaster have come

Left: Following the Walsingham Way

down, the laths exposed, but a clear-up is underway and I see that this is still a cared-for church with the feel of a simple chapel, and open for services.

A faint W has been scratched into the stone doorframe. Could that be a W for Walsingham? A green-painted iron money box cut into the wall has 'Free-Will Offer-ings' inscribed above the coin slot. There is no box for offerings made under duress.

Weeting to Mundford

Past the church the path skirts a very big pig farm – in which the pigs are having a lie in, snoring in unison – leaving the line of the Walsingham Way as it does so.

Once beyond the farm and back on the true path I find the old way incredibly at-mospheric. A place in which to feel, if not actually see, ghosts. We are treading in the footprints of countless thousands of pil-grims who came here over hundreds of years, and I feel the weight of history on my shoulders. Or perhaps that's my pack getting heavier the further I walk.

Pilgrim's Walk heads dart-straight north towards Walsingham. First on a broad track through forest then, in a sud-den downgrade, as a grassy path along a field margin. We have a thin belt of trees to our right, to our left a potato field, just sprouting, in which the light soil has been sculpted into the perfect, broad, flat-topped furrows.

Blomefield directly connects this path with the Walsingham Way. He writes: 'in the fields of Weeting north of the town is a Green Way called Walsingham Way, used (as 'tis said) by pilgrims on their way to the Lady of Walsingham... here was formerly a stone cross now broke into two pieces commonly called the Stump Cross.'

That cross was said to be at an ancient crossroads, where the north-bound Wals-ingham Way was bisected by an east-west route. It is possible that pilgrims from Ely would have joined the path here, guided – as were those from London – by that tow-ering stone beacon on the hillside sur-rounded by windswept heath.

Except that, today, the path marked on my map does not lead to the cross. Rather, it passes to the east of it, and we must di-vert for 500 yards west to find its remains, dwarfed by the forest that has grown up around it. Without the information board set at the side of the track I would never have found it. The board refers to 'The up-right stone in front of you' but all I can see is trees. We must trek along a faint path through the woods to find it, disguised like a forest version of Where's Wally? among trunks that ape it. I have been ex-pecting a couple of lengths of broken stone

Below: Searching for the Stump Cross

10

lying on the ground, so am pleasantly surprised to find a rough-hewn, lichen-cloaked shaft standing a good seven feet tall, firmly anchored in a square plinth.

The information board tells us the shaft originally stood 12ft and was topped with a cross, that it dates from the 1300s, and was snapped off either at the Reformation, in the 1530s, or in 1643 during the Parliamentary period.

It is also said that the hill the cross stands on is called Mount Ephraim, but that is actually to the east according to my OS map, at a point I pass once I have retraced my steps to the spot where the Pilgrim's Path ends abruptly.

So, clearly, history has muddled the facts. On an 1828 map of Norfolk there is a track leading on, north-easterly, from

Mount Ephraim to Mundford, but today the whole area is flooded with pine forest. I am drowning in trees. The true path is buried beneath them. However, we do know that it passed through the village of Ickburgh, 3½ miles or so north and just beyond Mundford. Now I must pick my way over a grid of forest tracks and fire breaks, moving one square east, one square north, in a game of pilgrim draughts, to emerge on the edge of Mundford. But, first, I say farewell to my fellow walkers who are looping back to Brandon.

Mundford to Ickburgh

Mundford is a lovely village. The stone tower of St Leonard's church is topped with a steeply pitched slate roof, from which a spire as sharp as a stiletto stabs at the heav-

Below: St Leonard's, Mundford

ens. On the village green is an inn, the *Crown*, dating from 1650 and a welcoming place for lunch, or to stay if you would like to split this stage over two days. Across the green is a village shop.

Half a mile beyond Mundford my route, now a rare pavement stretch along the A1065, crosses the River Wissey. There was once a pilgrim chapel and hospital here, dedicated to Our Lady and St Lawrence.

To the left of the road on the other side of the River Wissey, behind a tall brown fence, a part of that pilgrim facility survives as Bridge House. I step up onto a traffic barrier to peer over the fence at it. I see a pleasant flint house, several walls of which survive from what was a pilgrim hospital run by the Austin Friars, who offered care and accommodation for poor travellers and pilgrims.

It was common to build chapels on or beside bridges in the Middle Ages, and this one was maintained by a hermit, who was responsible for repairs to the bridge and sought alms from travellers. The river has been narrowed and its course shifted south since then, so it no longer runs directly past the house.

Ickburgh to Great Cressingham

From Ickburgh, pilgrims would have travelled on what is now the main road to the

ICKBURGH'S PILGRIM PAST

Our Lady and St Lawrence was founded in the 14th century, during the reign of Edward I. In 1409 it was referred to in a Papal Bull, or decree, from Pope Gregory XII who granted what was referred to as a 'lazar house' (a hospital for lepers) exemption from tithes on their 145 acres of land. It had probably been a hospital for some time, but by the 1450s, when leprosy had died out in the area, it appears to have ceased that function and to have catered solely for pilgrims and travellers.

Whatmore notes: 'The registers of the diocese of Norwich record several appointments to the joint office of hermit and chaplain at the bridge here.' From 1446 the hermit/chaplain was a John Lyster, who died in 1526 and 'desired to be buried in the church of Mundford and left 16 acres and other property to that parish'. Another hermit was named as 'good Richard of Cornwall' who was praised 'for his plain preaching against sin at Ickburgh.'

After the Reformation the chapel became a farmhouse and was later divided into a row of three cottages.

Above: Through the park to All Saints, Hilborough

next village, Hilborough, and I can't avoid that for a mile and a half, but only the middle third of that is on the verge. For the first third there is a pavement, for the last I can duck into the forest and follow the road at a more comfortable distance.

From the Desert Rats Memorial, where a tank stands on a brick plinth, I am able to tack north again, on another one-square-left, one-square-right progression along forest tracks. I do so to avoid both main road and the restricted military training grounds – marked 'Danger Area' on my map in angry red type – that combine to frustrate the pilgrim.

I make it to Hilborough, with just a further short stretch along a verge before pavement takes over. Once in the village I can turn my back on the road and take a footpath over meadows to my next pilgrim point. I can't resist a church isolated on a hill, and 14th century All Saints is just that. I climb through parkland spotted with a rash of brown molehills, skirting a mysterious hill-side hollow with brackish water

at the bottom, to reach the church. It has strong family connections with one of Norfolk's most famous sons: Lord Nelson, hero of the 1803-15 Napoleonic Wars between Britain and France. His father and grandfather were rectors here, and his sister, two elder brothers and other relatives are buried in the churchyard.

A bench in that churchyard bears the inscription 'Sit In The Sun'. So I do, and reflect on some of the most prominent pilgrims who have passed through Hilborough before me. Among them was Henry VI, who lived from 1421 to 1471 and who went three times to Walsingham, staying at Hilborough twice. He began from various starting points, but his pilgrim paths took in Bury St Edmunds, Thetford and Brandon. He also stopped at Pickenhamwade (now Pickenham) and Litcham, which I shall encounter in Stages 11 and 12.

I am hopeful of finding another pilgrim treasure in Hilborough: the site of a pilgrim chapel dedicated to St Margaret of Antioch. Its location is marked on my Ordnance Survey map, and Whatmore writes of 'the remains of a chapel in a field.' He says it was 'well endowed with 100 acres of land and had its own priests' but was 'dissolved along with all other "free" chapels and chantry chapels under Edward VI', Henry VIII's son. In the 18th century it was being used by a farmer to store hay.

I trek up Cockley Cley Rd on its trail. When I come alongside the spot where it ought to be, I peer through an unruly hedgerow to a marshy, reedy field that is being colonised by scrubby shrubs. Somewhere in there are the remains of the pilgrim chapel visited by Henry VI, but I can't for the life of me see it, and I can't get

Right: All Saints, Hilborough

into the field for a closer look.

So, sadly, for the first time on my pilgrim journey I must admit defeat. I try not to let it get me down as I follow the pavement though Hilborough to the Swan Inn, on the edge of the village. But my failure is still niggling me as I tramp the short stretch on the grass verge before I can leave the busy A1065 for quiet lanes that take me to Great Cressingham, and the Olde Windmill Inn.

It persists in bothering me as I relax, boots off, feet expanding in relief at their freedom, in the bar. I tell myself that this stage has actually delivered up a string of pilgrim discoveries: sacred spots that even centuries of neglect and wanton destruction have not been able to erase entirely, so I need to consider my glass half full, at least.

Above: The Olde Windmill Inn, Great Cressingham

10

Then I realise that my actual glass is a lot less than half full. So, remembering the Serenity Prayer, which teaches that we should learn to accept the things we can't change, and have the courage to change the things that we can, I put disappointment behind me and, empty glass and courage in hand, go up to the bar.

11

Great Cressingham to Castle Acre

Along the ancient Peddars Way – in the foot-steps of Katherine of Aragon – via an isolated hill-top church rescued from Satanists, to the last medieval pilgrim stop before Walsingham

The Peddars Way shuns villages, powering determinedly on at an unvarying elevation above the Wissey valley. It gives nothing but a brief wave to Houghton on the Hill, South Pickenham and South Acre, but churches at each demand a brief detour from me.

The Peddars Way – its name said to derive from the Latin *pedester*, meaning on foot – is at least Roman, possibly older, and may be an extension of the Icknield Way, which I touched upon on my way from Bury St Edmunds to Thetford. It first appeared on a map in 1587, but its credentials as a pilgrim route to Walsingham are impeccable.

This is rolling country – well, rolling for Norfolk – with insular villages tucked in folds in the valleys, away from main roads. My destination today is Castle Acre, a fortified Norman town at which many pilgrims from London would have spent their last night before arriving at Walsingham. I am conscious with each step that I am inching closer to my goal, and my pace quickens, along with my sense of anticipation.

Castle Acre Castle

PRACTICAL INFORMATION

ROUTE OVERVIEW   13.7 miles (22.1km)

This is a very rural section, with no towns along it, and no pubs or shops directly on the route. This limits options to spread this stage over two days, especially since the only pub at North Pickenham, the rough half-way point, was closed at the time of research and publication. The most practical option is either to leave the path at North Pickenham and walk to Swaffham (2.4 miles/3.9km off the route) or to follow the route for another 1.6 miles/2.6km to the A47 services and call a taxi to pick you up from there, returning the next morning.

You will follow the Peddars Way for almost the entire stage. From Great Cressingham it is a steady but comfortable climb by lane to join the Peddars Way, which runs as a quiet lane through a gentle descent to South Pickenham, reached in **2.9 miles**. St Mary's, Houghton on the Hill is another **1.4 miles** along the Peddars Way, shortly after which you follow it across country to descend to North Pickenham, reached in **2 miles**.

On the second half of the stage, the Peddars Way runs Roman-road straight, ascending steadily but comfortably to cross the A47 (in **2.3 miles**) then descending to South Acre (a further **4.2 miles**). The final stretch runs uphill to Castle Acre, reached in **0.9 miles**.

Public transport options

There are no towns or railway stations on this stage and only infrequent community **bus** services (No 12 between Swaffham & North Pickenham, and the No 32 Swaffham Flexibus via Castle Acre). See also public transport map and table pp29-31.

All villages along the path are accessible from Swaffham (1.5 miles/2.4km off route) by **taxi**. Try *Swaffham Taxis* (☎ 0800-6129063) or *Al's Cabs* (☎ 01760-720002).

Where to eat or stay along the way

● **Great Cressingham** (see Stage 10, p143)
● **North Pickenham** (after 6.7 miles, 10.8km) The only pub, The *Blue Lion* (☎ 01760-622527, 🖥 bluelion pub.com) was closed at time of research; check if this has reopened.
● **Swaffham** (**on foot** after 7 miles/11.3km then off route 2.4 miles/3.9km; **by taxi** from A47 services after 8.6 miles/13.9km then off route 1.5 miles/2.4km) Two friendly former coaching inns offer options to **stay** and **eat** here – there's the *Red Lion* (☎ 01760-721022,

---

● **Terrain** Following the Peddars Way along quiet lanes, tracks and footpaths over gently undulating country
● **Difficulty** Easy/moderate
● **Cumulative distance from London** 155.8 miles (251.1km)
● **Time** 4 hours 50 mins actual walking time   ● **Total ascent** 234m/767ft
● **Map** OS Explorer *236 King's Lynn, Downham Market & Swaffham*
● **GPX route file & directions*** 511.pdf, 511.gpx, 511.kml at 🖥 https://trailblazer-guides.com/press * See pp27-8 for more information on downloads

🖳 redlionswaffham.co.uk, 87 Market Pl; open Mon & Tue 6-10pm, Wed-Fri noon-3pm & 6-11pm, Sat noon-midnight, Sun noon-8pm, food Mon-Sat noon-8pm, Sun noon-6pm; 10 en-suite rooms) on the main square; and dating from 16th century, *The George* (☎ 01760-721238, 🖳 georgehotel-swaffham.co.uk, Station St; open from 11am, food daily noon-2.15pm, 6pm-9.30pm) has 28 en-suite rooms.

● **A47** (after 8.6miles/13.9km) Fast **food** is available at *Swaffham Services* (🖳 motor wayservices.uk/Swaffham) which has a McDonalds and the adjacent garage has Costa Coffee, snacks and toilets.

● **Sporle** (after 9.9 miles/15.9km, then off route 0.9 miles/1.4km) If passing through on a Sunday, treat yourself to **lunch** at *The Squirrel's Drey* (☎ 01760-788101, 🖳 squir relsdrey.co.uk, 70 The Street; Mon & Tue closed, food Wed-Sat 5.30pm-9.30pm, Sun noon-3pm), a small and cosy family-run pub and restaurant.

● **Castle Acre** With atmospheric **rooms** and good **food**, the 16th century *Ostrich Inn* (☎ 01760-755398, 🖳 theostrich.pub, Stocks Green; open Tue-Sun noon-10/11pm, Mon closed, food Tue-Sat noon-8pm, Sun noon to 6pm) is a former coaching inn overlooking the village green. Alternatively, former pub the *Old Red Lion* (☎ 01760-755557, 🖳 old redlion.org.uk; Bailey St) is now a **hostel** with private rooms and dormitories. For other **accommodation** options in and near the village see 🖳 castleacre.info/accommo dation.htm. **Takeaway food** is on offer at *Castle Acre Fish and Chips* (☎ 01760-755234; Tue-Fri noon-2pm, 4pm-8pm, Sat 11.30am-2pm, 4pm-8.30pm, Sun & Mon closed) is at Foxes Meadow, off Back Lane.

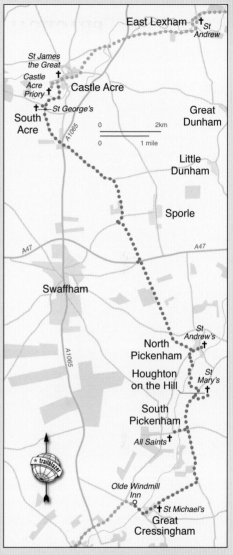

Services

● **Swaffham** has **supermarkets** Waitrose (Mon-Sat 7.30am-8pm, Sun 10am-4pm) on Castle Acre Rd, and Tesco (Mon-Sat 6am-10pm, Sun 10am-4pm) at 15 Brocks Rd.

● **Castle Acre** Stock up on essentials at **convenience store** Spar (Mon-Sat 6am-8pm, Sun 8am-6pm) on Back Lane.

PILGRIMAGE HIGHLIGHTS

- **Great Cressingham** *St Michael* (☎ 01366-328921 ⌨ achurchnearyou.com/church/10235, St Michael's Cres; open daily Apr-Sep, services check with church).
- **South Pickenham** *All Saints* (☎ 01760-722021 for rector or ☎ 01760-756360 for local keyholder, ⌨ achurchnearyou.com/church/4744, The Street; open by prior arrangement with keyholders, services occasional).
- **Houghton on the Hill** *St Mary* (☎ 01760-720070, ⌨ houghtonstmarys.co.uk, Peddars Way; open April-Oct daily 2-4pm, Nov-March Sat & Sun 2-4pm, other times by arrangement) **Pilgrim stamp in church.**
- **North Pickenham** *St Andrew* (☎ 01760 722021, ⌨ achurchnearyou.com/church/10244, Off Hillside; open for services Sun 10am.)
- **South Acre** *St George* (☎ 01760-338562 ⌨ achurchnearyou.com/church/5317, Finger Hill; open for private prayer Sun, Tue & Fri 9am-4pm, services 2nd Sun 6pm).

For pilgrim highlights in Castle Acre, see Stage 12 page 168

Great Cressingham to South Pickenham
It is just a short walk down the lane from the Olde Windmill, crossing the River Wissey, to Great Cressingham village. St Michael's church (**above**), its churchyard a carpet of primroses, is imposing, its great tower soaring skyward and topped with battlements and pinnacles. The remains of a late medieval statue of St Michael stand in a niche above the porch. Inside is a treasure house of 15th century glass. The windows of the north aisle feature a group of six bishops and two sequences of half a dozen angels. There are three fragmented representations of Christ, hard to make out, but I can see that one shows him rising from his tomb at the Resurrection.

I climb out of the Wissey valley up a narrow lane to the ridge along which the Peddars Way runs and turn left on the ancient path that will take me all the way to Castle Acre.

My OS Explorer map can't make up its mind about this route. Sometimes it shows it as a lane when it's a track, at others as a track when it's a lane. That fools the odd motorist, but is of no worry to the pilgrim, for the whole route is generally traffic-free as it lopes along.

Certainly nothing passes me as I walk towards South Pickenham, where I make my first short diversion. I had been in two minds whether the round-tower church of All Saints was worth dropping down off the Peddars Way for, but it holds something that intrigued me. When I telephoned, towards the end of lockdown, to ask if the church could be opened up for me I was told no one had been in it for months, so: 'I don't know what state you'll find it in.'

As I pushed open the heavy oak door I heard the cheeping of fledglings and saw the plastic sheeting covering the pews speckled with droppings. But there, in a gallery high above the nave, was a real treasure, not medieval this time but Victorian.

Its story is worth telling. In the mid-19th century Augustus Welby Northmore Pugin, famously the designer of the interiors of the Palace of Westminster and the Elizabeth Tower that closets Big Ben, rebuilt the church of St Mary, nine miles away at West Tofts, in grand neo-Gothic style. Among its treasures was a remarkable painted wooden organ casing.

During the Second World War, West Tofts was among six villages that fell within the Army's requisitioned, 300,000-acre Stanford battle training area. The population was removed and has never been al-

Below / right: All Saints South Pickenham and the organ.

lowed back. The church remains, but in the 1950s the organ was brought here.

And there it is, high above my head at the back of the church. The wings of the painted gold, red and green wooden casing, as bright as a fairground ride, open out to reveal gloriously rich and vivid images of the Nativity and the Adoration of the Magi. Across the gallery is written: 'Serve the Lord with gladness, and come before his presence with a song.'

South Pickenham to Houghton on the Hill

Back up on the Peddars Way, I walk above the valley in which the rich russet earth has just been turned ready for this year's crop, and on to my next treasure house: the wonderful rescued church of St Mary, at Houghton on the Hill.

At the roadside, tucked behind a hedge and easy to miss, is a black and white fingerpost pointing the way. It ought to say 'the finest church you will see all day'. If you didn't know it was above you on the ridge, hidden in the trees, you could pass by unawares. What a loss that would be. St Mary's has one of the most remarkable stories on the whole of my pilgrim path from London.

I climb to it up a track tucked beneath trees on the margin of the field that runs down to the Peddars Way. The church only reveals itself when I reach the summit and turn a corner to find it stand-

ing, in a wonderful sun-dappled garden glade, encircled in an embrace of trees.

There are flower beds, shrubs, and many memorial benches dotted about. The whole is lovingly tended. A place of contemplation, remembrance. There's even a very pilgrim-friendly shed with a sign: 'Toilet'.

St Mary's dates from at least 1090, perhaps even from the 7th century, when St Felix converted East Anglia to Christianity. It has been through many alterations in its long life, which have left it looking just a little disjointed.

Sitting alongside it in the garden, I have before me a little arched door that looks Saxon, beside a great oblong window that looks 18th century, topped with an orange tile roof that puts me in mind of a Norfolk cottage. The short, tall and narrow nave, a mix of flint, rubble and Roman brick, is attached to a tower that by rights ought to be part of a much bigger church. As it is, St Mary's looks a bit like a toddler with Popeye's arm.

Volunteers keep this church open two hours each afternoon and at other times by arrangement. Today it is Brian and Maureen who usher me in and talk me through the stories presented in 11th century wall

St Mary's, Houghton on the Hill (left) dates back to at least 1090 and contains superb Saxon wall paintings **(right)**.

paintings that were revealed when the church was being restored, and which cover the interior like a full-body tattoo. These are some of the most important late Saxon wall paintings in western Europe.

They were designed like a great picture book, a sort of cartoon strip telling the Bible stories of Heaven, Earth and Hell for those who could not read. The once vibrant colours are now faded to a uniform

BOB DAVEY, SAVIOUR OF ST MARY'S

Bob Davey's wife Gloria was walking with the Women's Institute in 1992 when she came across this church, its tower hidden behind a curtain of ivy, its interior desecrated by Satanists who had torn up graves, set up a pagan altar, and scratched the number 666 into a wall. The roof had fallen in and there was a serious crack in the tower. She told Bob, a churchwarden at the next village, North Pickenham, and he immediately started to reclaim the church from the devil worshippers, cutting down the ivy and planning a programme of repairs. For 25 years he laboured, shoring up the tower, rebuilding the walls, and replacing the original thatched roof with tile. The medieval font was discovered, being used as a garden planter, and returned.

Bob struggled to get interest in his restoration, and the funds to progress it. But then, in 1996, the church's fortunes changed when a piece of Victorian plaster fell from a wall to reveal the remarkable 1,000-year-old paintings beneath. Grants were awarded, the Prince of Wales visited, and Bob got an MBE.

The church is still consecrated, occasional services are held, and pilgrims – including those who are re-establishing the church's place on the route to Walsingham – are made very welcome.

orange, but I can make out the Creation of Eve, and angels raising souls from the grave. Other images are harder to interpret, but I see fragments of a Last Judgement, at its centre a huge Trinity. Parts of the journey to heaven and the flight to hell remain. God is on his throne, supporting the cross to which Christ is nailed.

This church's saviour was a local man called Bob Davey (see above). Bob died only a couple of months before my visit, at the age of 91 from Covid, and Brian and Maureen were still mourning him.

Houghton on the Hill to
North Pickenham

I walk back down the track to the lane and along it for a few hundred yards, but soon

the Peddars Way forsakes tarmac to take a zig-zag path to the valley floor as it drops across fields to leap the River Wissey and skirt North Pickenham. Another short diversion is needed to take in the village.

There is hidden history here. The present church is dedicated to St Andrew, but Whatmore tells of another, 'a chapel, dedicated to St Paul, with a hermitage attached and a holy well'. The chapel was to the north of the current church, and the well on the other side of Hillside, the road running roughly north to south through the village.

Sadly, I draw a blank trying to find any trace of chapel, hermitage or well. I ask locals, but they can only scratch their heads. The well still appeared on Ordnance Survey maps in the 1950s, but the site has since been built on. No matter. There are bound to be disappointments on a pilgrim route that was abandoned 500 years ago.

At least I can reflect upon the fact that Catherine of Aragon passed through the stretch I covered this morning, from South to North Pickenham, on 13 March 1517. Whatmore recounts that Charles Brandon, Duke of Suffolk, wrote to Henry VIII a few days later telling him he met the queen at 'Pykenham Wade' (Pykenham being Pickenham) on her way to Walsingham, and escorted her the rest of the way. The name Pykenham Wade also appears in the pilgrimage itinerary of Henry VI, and Whatmore speculates that there may have been a ford, or wade, rather than a bridge over the River Wissey at some point between South and North Pickenham.

Before heading on I take a quick peak at St Andrew's, tucked up a side-turning on the corner of an L-shaped back way behind the pub. Apart from its 14th century tower, it is an almost completely Victorian building, and is only open for services. So I move on.

Above: St Andrew's, North Pickenham

North Pickenham to Castle Acre

The Peddars Way, which I rejoin just outside the village, has a second name here: Procession Lane, which may be connected with its use by pilgrims processing towards Castle Acre. It runs dead straight between high hedges as it climbs out of the valley, and feels very Roman as it progresses, first as a lane then as a track, until

THE WALSINGHAM WAY ACCORDING TO WHATMORE

Leonard Whatmore, writing in his *Highway to Walsingham*, would have had us take a slightly different trajectory after North Pickenham. His research convinced him that the Walsingham Way would have run due north, rather than the slightly more westerly path I have taken. He estimates the road will have gone through Sporle Wood, which is marked on my OS map just east of the village of Sporle, and then through Little Dunham and Great Dunham to Litcham, leaving out Castle Acre altogether.

If he is right, then the old road he wants us to follow has left no trace. However, there is overwhelming documentary evidence that many pilgrims on the road from London did indeed go via Castle Acre. So I decide Leonard Whatmore and I should agree to differ, go our own ways for a while, and meet up again at Litcham, in Stage 12.

St George's, South Acre (**above**) and the Barkham Mausoleum (**below**).

pilgrim hostelry, perhaps, but a place to fuel up on coffee and fast food if you can't make it any further, or to split the route by summoning a taxi to nearby Swaffham.

Then its lane/track/lane again dead straight over the Bartholomew Hills, followed by a descent to cross the A1065, a road that's been shadowing my progress since Brandon, and a climb and short diversion to another village, South Acre.

St George's in South Acre is another church worthy of the short detour needed to get to it. A quick climb up a shady lane from the Peddars Way has me in a village of just a few houses, clustered around another fine church. St George's has a Norman font with a soaring 16th-century canopy – like a sort of gothic, three-tiered wedding cake – which draws my eye up to the beautiful hammer-beam roof. At its

it is rudely interrupted by the A47. It's quite a shock to encounter the modern world again after the best part of a day in the heart of the country.

But just to the left is a roundabout with islands that help the pilgrim cross this busy road, and on the other side a service station with a McDonalds. Not your ideal

upper tier it has a series of delicately carved flying buttresses around an inner octagonal core, on which some of the green and red medieval paint has survived, and it is topped with a crown 'of pierced tracery carvings' to quote the church guide. It's a lovely, elegant thing.

At the east end of the north aisle, beside the sanctuary, is an elaborate alabaster and marble tomb, the 17th century Barkham Mausoleum, protected behind a wrought iron screen. On top of the tomb chest are carvings of Sir Edward Barkham, a former Lord Mayor of London who died in 1623, and his wife, Penelope.

Above the chest is a wall piece with representations of the figure of life – in the shape of a young girl – and death as a shrouded, tombstone-toothed skeleton, plus an hourglass with gilded wings (which is a very elegant way of saying 'time flies'). Below Edward and

Penelope, on the face of the chest, their children kneel in mourning, flanking a panel depicting a charnel cage crowded with skulls.

There is a squint, an angled slot in the wall, giving a letterbox view of the altar from the north aisle.

Perhaps the most charming feature in the church is the quirky collection of creatures carved into the poppy-head ends to the choir pews. They date from the last century, and I count among them a snail, a frog, a dolphin, a fish and an otter with a fish in its mouth.

There is a pilgrim here too, in effigy: a 12th-century Knight Templar in stone.

I retrace my steps to rejoin the Peddars Way. From here the lane whirls round clockwise and drops fast to the river and the final approach to Castle Acre, where a view of the priory ruins spurs me on.

A sign by a ford warns of 'Deep Water'. But not for us pilgrims. A footbridge takes me over the swirling waters of the River Nar. Not so the BMW driver who I pass, his car pulled up at the edge of the water, standing by the river and looking at the flow. I suppress the urge to will him on. The water looks a good three feet deep, and a match even for a combination of German engineering and youthful bravado.

Once across, I am on the very edge of Castle Acre Priory grounds. Before me, the remains of what was a massive religious house are laid out on a sloping meadow that is a riot of wild flowers. Alongside it the tower of the church of St James the Great rises above the trees in the heart of the village. I pause to drink in the scene before leaning in to the final, sharply up-hill climb straight to the village, and today's finishing line.

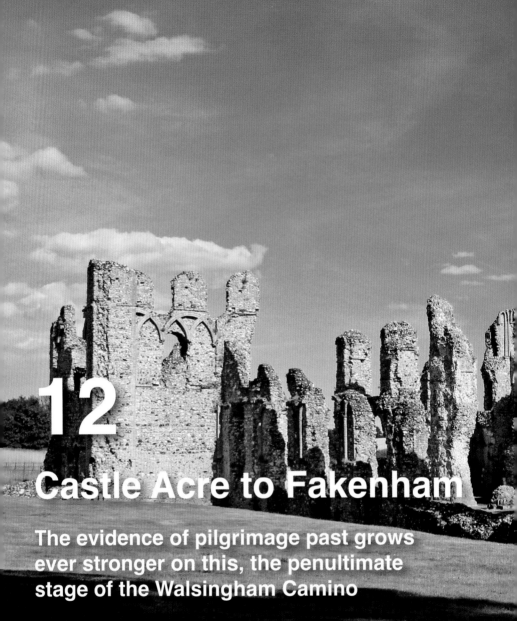

12

Castle Acre to Fakenham

The evidence of pilgrimage past grows ever stronger on this, the penultimate stage of the Walsingham Camino

After all the ruinous remains of pilgrim priories that have lined my route from London, it is a relief to find here, at Castle Acre, something that is still standing and which medieval pilgrims might recognise.

It's not complete, by any means, but the west front of Castle Acre Priory, through which medieval pilgrims entered the priory church

still stands, a sheet of stone rather like a stage-scenery flat. I fear for its stability in the face of Norfolk gales, but it is anchored to the earth at one end by the surviving quarters of the prior and has, I reassure myself, been standing since 1160. For those on horseback, this would have been the last overnight stop before Walsingham, but that is 21

12

miles away and, as I ride Shanks's pony, I'm going to rest at Fakenham tonight, six miles short of my final destination.

On the way I shall encounter several more very solid survivors from medieval times, including another important priory beside the River Nar at Litcham, where pilgrims from King's Lynn joined those from London for the final leg to Walsingham, and an 1100-year-old round tower church at East Lexham, one of the oldest in England.

PRACTICAL INFORMATION

ROUTE OVERVIEW   15.9 miles (25.6km)
Options to divide this stage are limited. At around 5.5 miles (8.8km) in on today's 15.9 mile stage, Litcham is nowhere near half way, but it does have an inn and a grocery, so is a good place to stock up. Tittleshall is at the half-way point, but has no facilities. See below for taxis covering the route.

From Castle Acre the route follows the Nar Valley Way on a level path close to the river, before a short gentle climb up a lane to East Lexham, reached in **3.7 miles**. Quiet roads take you on to Litcham, in **1.9 miles**, the most substantial village on the stage. It is **2.9 miles** more on level lanes to Tittleshall, the half-way point.

Whissonsett is a further **2.4 miles**, mainly on footpaths, and it is **2.5 miles** more to Colkirk, once again on quiet lanes. Fakenham is reached in another **2.5 miles**.

Public transport options
Again, you are deep in the countryside here. Other than the infrequent No 32 community **bus** between Castle Acre and Litcham, the only viable transport option on this stage is a **taxi**. Among operators are *Tiny's Taxis* (☎ 01328-888888, 🖥 www.tinys.org.uk) and *Jak's Taxis* (☎ 01328-887488, 🖥 jaktaxis.co.uk), both based in Fakenham. See also pp29-31.

Where to eat or stay along the way
● **Castle Acre** (see Stage 11, p155)

● **Terrain** Following footpaths and quiet lanes over very flat country
● **Difficulty** Moderate
● **Cumulative distance from London** 171.6miles (276.4km)
● **Time** 5 hours 30 mins actual walking time
● **Total ascent** 218m/715ft
● **Maps** OS Explorer: *238 Dereham & Aylsham, 251 Norfolk Coast Central*
● **GPX route file & directions*** 512.pdf, 512.gpx, 512.kml at 🖥 https://trailblazer-guides.com/press * See pp27-8 for more information on downloads

● **Litcham** (after 5.5 miles, 8.8km) **Stay** and **eat** at *Bull Inn* (☎ 01328-701340; check with pub for current opening and food hours; 1 Church St), a village inn with rooms.
● **Godwick** (after 9.6 miles 15.4km) *Godwick Hall* (☎ 01328-701948, 🖳 godwick hall.co.uk, Mill Lane; 2 nights minimum) is a possible **accommodation** point if you are prepared to splash out on one of its three swanky shepherds huts.
● **Fakenham Accommodation** options include *Wensum Lodge Hotel* (☎ 01328-862100, 🖳 wensumlodge.co.uk; Bridge St; 17 en-suite rooms) by the river and part of a former mill dating from 1750; and *Erika's B&B* (☎ 01328 863058, 🖳 erikas-bandb.co.uk; 3 Gladstone Rd NR21 9BZ) six en-suite rooms in a modern house close to the town centre. For a **meal** head to *The Crown* (☎ 01328-855278, 🖳 facebook .com & search The Crown Fakenham; 6 Market Pl; open Mon-Sat 10am-late, Sun from 11am, food Mon-Wed noon-2pm, Thur-Sat noon-2pm & 6-9pm, Sun carvery noon-3pm), a friendly, 15th-century local and former pilgrim hostelry.

Services
● **Litcham** *Post office Stores* (☎ 0345-7223344; open Mon-Sat 7.30am-7pm, Sun 9am-1pm; Church St PE32 2NS) grocery with in-store bakery.
● **Fakenham** *Aldi* (Norwich Rd; Mon-Sat 8am-10pm, Sun 10am-4pm); *The Larder wholefoods store* (☎ 01328-855306, 10 Norwich St; Mon-Sat 9am-5pm, Sun closed.)

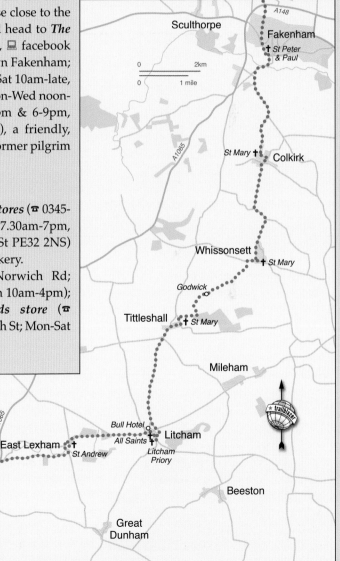

PILGRIMAGE HIGHLIGHTS

- **Castle Acre** *Priory* (🖳 english-heritage.org.uk, Priory Rd; open daily summer 10am-5pm, check website for winter variations) Maintained by English Heritage.
- **Castle Acre** *St James the Great* (☎ 01760-338562, 🖳 achurchnearyou.com/church/5313, Stocks Green; open daily10am-4pm, services Sun 10.30am), contact church regarding services for the patron saint's day, 25 July. **Pilgrim stamp in church.**
- **East Lexham** *St Andrew*, (🖳 achurchnearyou.com/church/10263, off Lexham Rd; open daily dawn to dusk, no services)
- **Litcham** *Priory* now a private house, but visible from the road (Church St)
- **Litcham** *All Saints* (☎ 01328-700765, 🖳 achurchnearyou.com/church/10265, Church St; open 9am-6pm, services Sun 10.15am).
- **Tittleshall** *St Mary the Virgin* (☎ 01328-701011, 🖳 achurchnearyou.com/church/10273, Church Lane; open 9am-4pm, services contact church for details)
- **Godwick** (☎ 01328-701948, 🖳 lostvillageofgodwick.co.uk, Mill Lane; open Mon, Tue, Thur & Fri dawn to dusk, Sat dawn to noon, Wed & Sun closed, visible from footpath at other times) abandoned medieval village.
- **Whissonsett** *St Mary* (☎ 01328-853226, 🖳 achurchnearyou.com/church/10278, off High St; open daily 10am-4pm, services 1st and 3rd Sun 10.30am)
- **Colkirk** *St Mary* (☎ 01328-853226, 🖳 achurchnearyou.com/church/10255, Church Rd; open/services check website).

For pilgrim highlights in Fakenham, see Stage 13, page 180

Castle Acre

Castle Acre is a magical place: a Norman walled village with priory at one end, castle at the other, and a huddle of houses around the central green. It even has a gatehouse standing astride the main road into the town.

Above: The prior's house, Castle Acre Priory

I start my exploration at Castle Acre Priory, imagining myself in the shoes of a medieval pilgrim preparing to enter the priory church through the western doorway. But first I pause to take in the substantial building that survives before me. The west face itself stands tall, although the niches that cover it have been stripped of the statues of saints. Above them is the great empty eye of the west window. To the right of the church, their two storeys still intact, are the prior's lodgings, with a large hall, great chamber and chapel on the first floor. I step inside and explore. This section survived the Dissolution, when the rest of the priory was stripped and gutted, because it was easily adapted as a nobleman's house.

Above: Ruins of Castle Acre Priory

I return to the church and walk through the empty doorway, up the nave to the transept and on through the quire to the sanctuary. Yellow wallflowers have colonised the stonework, clinging in clusters to the sheer walls that rise above me.

Leaving the church to my right I can walk clockwise around the cloister, past the chapter house to the monks' dormitory, and on past the refectory on the southern arm to the western walkway. Pilgrims would have stayed here, in the guest hall on the first floor overlooking the cloister. At least, the well-heeled ones would have. This was a grand hall. That and its proximity to the prior's own lodgings suggest that any pilgrims given shelter here would have been high status. We know that Henry III was among them, as were Edward I and his queen, Eleanor. Aristocrats, priors and abbots were also made welcome.

I walk from the priory to the church of St James the Great. One of the churchwardens, Anne Loch, who is just refreshing the flowers when I pop in, breaks off to tell me of the wonderful services they hold for pilgrims to mark their patron's saint's day, on 25 July. She points out the church's many treasures, starting with the font, its dart-

like 15th century oak cover soaring like a fretworked spire towards the roof. Cleverly, it can be raised and lowered thanks to a mechanism of counterweights like that in a sash window. At the pinnacle a golden dove flies. Anne apologises for the cobweb strung across its wings. They simply don't have a duster with a long enough handle. Who does? It would take a fire engine's telescopic ladder to reach that far.

Above: Church of St James, Castle Acre

Then there is the 15th century wine-glass pulpit, with painted wood panels, and the surviving lower section of the rood screen, on which St James the Great, with his scallop shell and staff, appears alongside the other apostles. In the guidebook the Canon Rector, Stuart Nairn notes: 'It is appropriate that he should be the patron of the church in a village with a Cluniac priory, as Cluniac monks were great supporters of pilgrimages to Compostela'. The rest of the screen is gone, but the stairway to the rood loft, which

would have supported the crucifix, still corkscrews up inside the wall, inviting exploration.

Finally, there is the Lady Chapel where, on the altar, a dusky Mary dressed in blue stands, with Christ in a gold sleepsuit in her arms.

Leaving, I pass a board offering an encouraging message for a pilgrim: 'Thank you for visiting, go safely on your way'. I walk on, along the quiet village street and past the green, around which there would once have been dozens of pilgrim hostelries, rather than the one that survives today.

The Church of St James, Castle Acre, contains medieval gems that would have been seen by pilgrims at the time including the font and heavy font cover (**above**) and the rood screen (**below**).

CASTLE ACRE HISTORY

Castle Acre was developed after the Norman Conquest by William de Warenne, who rather shrewdly married William the Conqueror's daughter, Gundrada. He was made Earl of Surrey, and also given land here. In 1079 he brought French monks from the abbey at Cluny and, as their abbey rose to the west, his mansion, the castle which gives the village its name, was built in the east.

Halfway between priory and castle, the Surreys built the church of St James the Great in the late 12th or early 13th century. It may be that the original priory church stood here.

The Cluniac order were renowned as pilgrim hosts, and it so happened that the priory was ideally placed on the road to the Holy House at Walsingham, the most important shrine in England. As pilgrimage there grew in popularity from the 11th century, so did the power of this priory. It was built to house only 30 monks, but is massive, indicating its importance.

At the Reformation it was given to Thomas Howard, Duke of Norfolk and later passed through several families until bought by Edward Coke of Holkham Hall. It is still owned by the Cokes, who became the Earls of Leicester and whose name will crop up again during this stage.

Castle Acre to Litcham

I leave the Peddars Way as I depart Castle Acre and pick up the Nar Valley Way, running north east to the next village, East Lexham. My path follows a green way, sunken between hedgerows that close overhead to form a green tunnel. The route shadows the River Nar before joining a quiet lane to cross over it at Newton Mill, the waters rushing beneath the bridge and around a tiny island on which a swan has built its nest.

I abandon the Nar Valley Way and join another lane for the final climb away from the river to East Lexham. I can see, over to my right, a farmyard within which stands the remarkable round-tower church of St Andrew. The rough-hewn tower, like a sandcastle patted into shape by childrens'

Above: The Saxon tower of the Church of St Andrew, East Lexham.

Above: Richard Forster's *The Nativity*;
Church of St Andrew, East Lexham

hands, rises from a cauldron of foaming pink blossom.

This is among the oldest churches in the country, and the most loved. The tower was built in around 900, and the circular churchyard, on which sheep are grazing, suggests it was a site of pagan worship before Christianity came to East Anglia in the 7th century.

St Andrew's holds ancient treasures. In the sanctuary stands a chair fashioned from three misericords – the flip-up seats that allowed infirm monks to rest their weary bones during Mass and Divine Office – which are believed to have been rescued from Castle Acre Priory at the Dissolution. But, for me, among the greatest treasures are the newest: three wall paintings by Richard Forster, who spent his early childhood at Church Farm

House, just across the farmyard, and who is now president of the Royal Society of Portrait Painters. For years, as he says in a leaflet I pick up in the church, he had felt that the blocked-off gothic window arch to the right of the sanctuary deserved a painting. In 2015 he created *The Nativity* to fill it. He went on to fill another niche, to the right of the altar, with a portrait of the church's patron, St Andrew. Behind the Jacobean altar is a third work, *The Rising From The Dead*, a bucolic resurrection scene set in a country churchyard similar to the one here.

From St Andrew's a quiet lane takes me along a tree-shaded avenue, the sheep-dotted pastures on my right dropping down to the smooth-flowing River Nar. I imagine well-heeled medieval pilgrims from Kings Lynn being rowed along here on their way to Litcham.

Litcham to Tittleshall

Like Castle Acre, Litcham was a key staging post for medieval Walsingham pilgrims and, once again, there is very solid evidence of that connection in the village. To find it I must walk down the main street of this busy, vibrant place, with its inn, general store and post office, butcher and school, to the point at which pilgrims who arrived by river would disembark.

On the way I visit All Saints, which has a fascinating set of medieval graffiti, cut into the pillars lining the nave in the 15th and early 16th centuries, and discovered beneath subsequent centuries' application of lime wash. The Norfolk Medieval Graffiti Survey identified symbols including the Pelta design or Solomon's Knot, a symbol used in the medieval church to ward off evil spirits, and dating from Roman times.

LITCHAM PRIORY

Leonard Whatmore, in his *Highway to Walsingham*, writes of a wooden cross, a navigational aid to medieval pilgrims, that stood beside the river in Litcham. There was a hermitage on the bridge, with a chapel beside it, and a 'house of rest for pilgrims on the road to Walsingham'. It is here that Whatmore has the pilgrim route from London crossing the river and being joined by the route from Kings Lynn.

The 17th century Priory Farmhouse **(right)** was 'built into the remains of the chapel to a hermitage. The foundations are those of the original chapel, and the east wall, with double buttresses at the angles, are those of the original pilgrims' chapel'. That wall, which the house presents to the road, has niches that are clearly ecclesiastical and, in the yard, there are stretches of priory wall between modern brick and a cottage called Pilgrims.

This farmhouse was the home of Matthew Halcott (or Holcott), a master tanner who, in his will of 23 September 1683, made a bequest of 'le chappell-house [and] le Hermitage' at Litcham and another property that is described as 'abutting on the Walsingham Way.'

Matthew is well commemorated in Litcham. He is portrayed on the village sign, which stands just across from All Saints Church. In 1668 he paid for the building of a new red brick and flint church tower, in thanksgiving for the restoration of Charles II to the throne.

The most intriguing graffiti, known as the Litcham Cryptogram, believed to have been cut by a Walsingham pilgrim, is hard to decipher and open to various interpretations, but one is that the top line of lettering, 'a s .j. m a y', stands for 'anima salv. jesu. maria a yosephu' which translates as 'save (my) soul Jesus, Mary and Joseph'. The first two letters of the lower line, 'm m', may refer to 'memento mori': remember you must die, but the meaning of the rest of the line, 'wyke

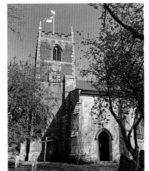

Above: Litcham Church

baumburgh' is pretty much anyone's guess. But I do wonder, is Baumburgh a reference to modern day Bamburgh, home of the warrior-king and Northern Saint, Oswald, and close to the holy island of Lindisfarne? Could this graffiti-artist have travelled by sea down the coast from Northumberland and then up the Nar, to disembark here?

I head on to Priory Farmhouse (see above), which stands at the foot of the village on the banks of the Nar.

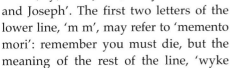

12

Above: Church of St Mary, Tittleshall

From Litcham the Walsingham Camino path forges north to Tittleshall, and I follow it on a quiet lane through land so flat that it seems squeezed to a sliver beneath the weight of the great blue bell jar of sky.

The weathervane swinging in the breeze above the tower of St Mary the Virgin in Tittleshall has a sheep on it. This was indeed sheep country, and the inhabitants got rich on their woolly backs, or at least some did.

Tittleshall was the home village of the post-Reformation owner of Castle Acre Priory, the great lawyer and rival of Francis Bacon, Sir Edward Coke. There is a memorial to him in the church. Sir Edward, who lived from 1552-1634, was exceedingly well connected, and in a perfect position after the Dissolution to buy up great tracts of land owned by religious orders and cathedrals, which he flooded with sheep, and made his fortune.

In his role as attorney general, Sir Edward prosecuted the Earl of Essex, Sir Walter Raleigh, Guy Fawkes and his Gunpowder Plotters. He became Chief Justice under James I.

The manor of Tittleshall was Coke's first purchase, in 1578, and he went on to buy Holkham, on the coast beyond Walsingham, and other estates. Cokes were buried here until they built a family mausoleum at Holkham Hall, their grand 18th century mansion, in the 1870s.

Tittleshall to Whissonsett

From Tittleshall I take a footpath across the fields to the remains of another Coke village, Godwick, abandoned in the 1600s. All that survives today is the tower of All Saints' Church, the Great Barn and the remains of Coke's house, Godwick Hall.

From here, the path follows what was once a lane leading to the next village, Whissonsett. The church, St Mary's, stands at the foot of a very long drive through a churchyard that is more paddock than graveyard. In a niche above the door stands a simple ceramic statue of the Virgin and Child, there to offer a pilgrim welcome. Inside is an ancient treasure: the head of a very rare 10th-century Anglo Saxon Cross, which was uncovered by grave diggers in the churchyard in 1902.

Most such crosses were broken up and used as building material when the Normans undertook the wholesale rebuilding of almost every church in England. This one, which dates from around 920, survived because it had fallen over in the churchyard and been covered by turf.

A prayer is suggested here, which seems entirely appropriate for a pilgrim now just a day from Walsingham. It reads:

'I stand before the Holy Mandala of
Christ's Risen Glory
I kneel before the Majesty of
Heaven's Holy Power
I acknowledge my frailty
I look to Divinity's all-encompassing Holding

Left: St Mary's, Whissonsett

I leave my burdens here
I go my way with a knowledge of the
Higher Grace
That shall bring all things to pass
In Perfect Time
As All is meant to be'

Whissonsett to Fakenham

I come across a material sign that I am getting close to Walsingham in the next village, Colkirk, where, in the Lady Chapel of 12th century St Mary the Virgin, I find a little statue of Our Lady of Walsingham, the Christ Child on her lap. It's a sweet, simple and affecting image and bears a note on brown card commemorating its placing here in 2019, and the words 'Our Lady of Peace'. This is the third church in a row dedicated to Mary, which I take as another sign that the Marian shrines at Walsingham are now very close. And, with this statue and the lines at Whissonsett, I feel that the prayers are rising up around me.

Colkirk is on the crest of what counts as a hill in Norfolk: standing on a 250ft eminence that rises from the river Wensum, two miles to the north. In medieval times, before this land was drained, the route I am following would have offered a safe, dry passage through the Fens for pilgrims.

I walk along lanes bisecting fields (**below**) that are a smear of vivid, Van Gogh yellow to skirt Pudding Norton, another abandoned medieval village, where the ruined tower of St Margaret's Church protrudes like a broken tooth above the hedgerows. On the outskirts of Fakenham, I pass the remains of an Augustinian priory founded as a hospital in the 12th century and dedicated to St Stephen, but now little more than bumps in the grass. Once, many pilgrims would have found shelter here. Today, I must wind on over the River Wensum and pick one of the pubs or B&Bs in the market town of Fakenham.

It is mid-afternoon, and I am tempted to press on to Walsingham, but restrain myself. Anticipation is, after all, half the joy of pilgrimage, and I want to arrive at my ultimate destination fresh and alert.

13
Fakenham to Walsingham

The final, glorious approach
to England's Nazareth

This is it. The final day. A short walk to England's greatest medieval pilgrim destination. Our Rome, our Jerusalem, our Santiago de Compostela. It is devotion to Mary, mother of Jesus, mother of us all, that brings pilgrims to Walsingham and hence, by extension and at its simplest, Walsingham is a place to venerate, and celebrate, motherhood.

Medieval pilgrims were drawn by a fantastical tale. In 1061, follow-ing a vision, Walsingham noblewoman Lady Richeldis de Faverches built a replica of the Holy Family's house in Walsingham. The Holy House, later richly ornamented with gold and precious jewels, be-came a shrine and attracted pilgrims to Walsingham from all over

Calvary, the Anglican Shrine; Walsingham

Europe. It was completely destroyed at the time of the Dissolution, but its site is marked in the grounds of the ruined Walsingham Abbey. Today, this is once again England's most important holy shrine, drawing 300,000 pilgrims every year.

I think of Henry VIII as I approach East Barsham, a place where he is known to have stayed on one of his many pilgrimages to Walsingham. I ponder, as I walk, how a man who held the Holy House at Walsingham Priory in such reverence, and showered it with such riches, could have turned against it so profoundly that he sought to erase it from the earth. For what reason, ultimately? The want of a wife who could bear him a healthy son? On such personal tribulations are profound changes wrought, if you happen to be a king.

PRACTICAL INFORMATION

ROUTE OVERVIEW   6.2 miles (10km)

This final short stage leaves plenty of time to immerse yourself in all that Walsingham has to offer the 21st century pilgrim, with plenty of facilities at the start and end of the walk.

It's a steady climb on pavements, and a final footpath stretch, from St Peter and St Paul church in Fakenham to reach the edge of town where, after **1.1 miles**, you cross the A148. A quiet lane takes you to a stretch on the B1105, followed by further lanes, dropping gently down to the village of East Barsham, reached in a further **2.3 miles**. Just beyond East Barsham, a steady climb along the verge is followed by a descent on a footpath over fields to North Barsham (**0.9 miles**).

Another quiet lane leads to the Slipper Chapel, the Catholic Shrine, in Houghton St Giles (**0.4 miles**). A footpath on an old railway track takes you on a gently rising, then falling, gradient for **0.9 miles** to the edge of Walsingham. Here a farm lane drops down to the B1105, High St, running through the village to reach the Anglican Shrine in **0.6 miles**.

Public transport options

This final stage is short but if you need a **bus** between Fakenham and Walsingham there's the hourly No 36 Coastliner. For your journey home from Walsingham, the nearest **train** stations are in King's Lynn or Norwich. To reach King's Lynn from Walsingham, take the

---

- **Terrain** Mainly quiet country lanes over gently undulating countryside
- **Difficulty** Easy ● **Cumulative distance from London** 177.9 miles (286.7km)
- **Time** 2hrs 15 mins actual walking time ● **Total ascent** 115m/378ft
- **Map** OS Explorer 251 *Norfolk Coast Central*
- **GPX route file & directions*** 513.pdf, 513.gpx, 513.kml at 🖳 https://trailblazer-guides.com/press *See pp27-8 for more information on downloads

northbound No 36 bus which travels there on a scenic route (approx 2hrs) round the North Norfolk coast. Alternatively, take the southbound No 36 back to Fakenham (15 mins) to pick up the X29 bus to Norwich (approx 1hr 30mins). See also public transport map and table pp29-31.

For a **taxi** try *Tiny's Taxis* (☎ 01328-888888, 🖳 www.tinys.org.uk) and *Jak's Taxis* (☎ 01328-887488, 🖳 jaktaxis.co.uk).

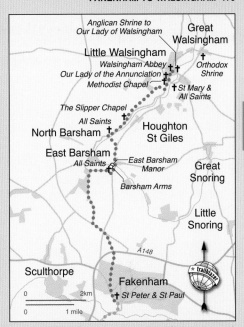

Where to eat or stay along the way

● **Fakenham** (see Stage 12, p167)
● **East Barsham** (after 3.5 miles, 5.6km) **Stay** and **eat** at *Barsham Arms* (☎ 01328-820729, 🖳 thebarshamarms.co.uk, Fakenham Rd; Tue-Sat noon-11pm, Sun noon-5pm, food Tue-Sat noon-2.30pm & 5-8.30pm, Sun 9am-5pm), a pub with rooms.

● **Walsingham Catholic Shrine accommodation** (☎ 01328 820 495, 🖳 walsingham.org .uk) Two complexes, Elmham House and Dowry House in Walsingham, plus shepherds' huts.
● **Walsingham Anglican Shrine accommodation** (☎ 01328-820239, 🖳 walsingham anglican.org.uk) A mix of accommodation within the shrine grounds, plus nearby cottages.
● **Walsingham Stay** at the very pleasant *Black Lion Hotel* (☎ 01328-820235, 🖳 blacklionhotelnorfolk.co.uk, Friday Market Pl; open Sun-Thur 11am-10.30pm, Fri & Sat to 11pm; food: Mon-Sat noon-3pm & 6-9pm, Sun noon-8pm), with impressive restaurant and six rooms on a quiet square; or *The Bull* (☎ 01328-820333, 🖳 thebullwalsingham.co .uk, 8 Common Pl; open Mon-Sat 8am-10.30pm, Sun to 10pm, food noon-9pm), a lively pub with six rooms. For B&B, *The Old Bakehouse B&B* (☎ 01328-820377; 33 High St) has three en-suite double or twin rooms. For more options: see 🖳 walsinghamvillage.org.
● **Walsingham Eat and drink** at the Anglican Shrine's *Norton Café Bar* (🖳 walsingham anglican.org.uk/visit/the-refectory; open Feb-Nov Mon-Sat 9am-11pm, Sun to 10.30pm, Dec-early Feb 9am-4.40pm), open all day for everything from a full English breakfast to lunch or supper. Or there's quirky *Read and Digest* (☎ 01328-821332, 54 High St; open Thur-Tue 10.30am-4pm), a café and second-hand bookshop; and *Victorious Bistro* (☎ 01328-820921, 🖳 victoriouswalsingham.com, 2 Wells Rd; Tue-Sat 9am-8pm).

Services

● **Fakenham** (see Stage 12, p167)
● **Walsingham** For the essentials there's useful **convenience store** *Walsingham Village Stores* (☎ 01328-820543, 🖳 walsinghamvillage.org, 25 High St; daily 7am-7pm), while Walsingham **Farm Shop** (☎ 01328-821877, 🖳 walsingham.co/our-farm-shops, Guild St; Mon-Sat 9am-5pm, Sun 10am-4pm) sells local produce, some from Walsingham Estate.

13

PILGRIMAGE HIGHLIGHTS

- **Fakenham** *St Peter and St Paul* (☎ 01328-862268, 🖳 fakenhamparishchurch.org .uk, Upper Market; open daily, services Sun 9.30 am, also 2nd Sun 8am).
- **East Barsham** *All Saints* (☎ 01328-821316, 🖳 achurchnearyou.com/church/ 10279, Fakenham Rd; open daily, service 3rd Sun 10am).
- **North Barsham** *All Saints* (☎ 01328-821316, 🖳 achurchnearyou.com/church/ 10280, Green Way; closed).
- **Walsingham** *Slipper Chapel, Catholic National Shrine* (☎ 01328 820217, 🖳 walsingham.org.uk, Houghton St Giles; open 10.30am-4pm, check website for current numerous Mass times) **Pilgrim Stamp in Slipper Chapel shop.**

Walsingham Abbey (☎ 01328 820510, 🖳 walsinghamabbey.com, Common Place; open Mon 11am-3.30pm, Tue-Sun 11am-4pm). For pilgrim group bookings 🖳 walsinghamabbey.com/groups-pilgrimage. **Pilgrim Stamp in ticket office.**

Anglican Shrine (☎ 01328-820255, 🖳 walsinghamanglican.org.uk, 2 Common Pl; open 7am-10pm, numerous services: see website). To arrange a pilgrimage: 🖳 walsinghamanglican.org.uk/visit/arrange-a-pilgrimage. **Pilgrim Stamp in reception.**

Orthodox Shrine (☎ 01328-820610, Station Rd; open Sat-Wed 2pm-4pm).

Methodist Chapel (🖳 walsinghammethodist.com; off High St), check website for current opening hours and events for pilgrims.

St Mary and All Saints (☎ 01328-821316, 🖳 walsinghamparishes.org.uk/calendar, Back Lane; open, check with church, services Sun 11am, plus others as listed on website) Anglican parish church.

Our Lady of the Annunciation (☎ 01328-713044, 🖳 catholicparishofwalsingham .org, Friday Market; open daily but check with church, Mass: Mon-Sat 9.30am, Sun 11am). Catholic parish church.

Fakenham to East Barsham

Fakenham's church of St Peter and St Paul (**right**) peers down at me from above the terrace of orange-brick shops that have been built with their backs to it. I get to it up an alley from the Market Place, and cross a churchyard corralled with high, black-iron railings. An area of recent memorials lies beneath a magnolia that sheds its creamy leaves over the little bunches of flowers, like confetti of remembrance.

It's a welcoming place. A tear-shaped, red, white and blue arrangement of cornflowers, roses and dahlias stands before the sanctuary, the altar backed with a lovely reredos of saints.

This church once marked another key point on the pilgrim road to Walsingham. Whatmore records a long list of the saints venerated here, all of whom had a candle burning permanently in their honour. They included St

Peter and St Paul, the church's twin patrons; St Mary, and at least 11 more. There were chapels to Mary, to St Thomas of Canterbury and others. In addition, a candle burned for Henry VI, a Walsingham pilgrim in 1455. He was a troubled king who died, deposed, in the Tower of London, but was considered a martyr and unofficial saint by many after his death.

Many pilgrims paused in Fakenham. Of the three pilgrim inns – the *Crown*, Lion, and Swan – the first survives as a pub.

I want a full day to experience Walsingham, so am up early for the climb out of town, then over the A148 for a brief stint on the B1105 before escaping onto the quiet lanes medieval pilgrims would have taken. Alternatively, you could stick to Fakenham Rd and travel more directly, but there is no pavement and the road can be busy. Much better to wind your way along the back lanes to East Barsham.

East Barsham

In East Barsham I enter the sacred space around Walsingham. From here, medieval

All Saints Church, East Barsham

pilgrims proceeded with great reverence.

The lane brings me out at the church of All Saints, tucked in beside Fakenham Rd on a tree-sheltered mound, the graveyard full of wildflowers – daffodils just giving way to bluebells when I visit.

This is the remnant of a once-larger church, reduced to a stump after the Dissolution. The short, squat nave has two great gothic arched windows on either side that are far too big for it, as if it has its eyes wide open. A pitched-tile roof above the porch caps what once would have been a tall tower. Inside it is a very organic place, lime plaster gently crumbling, the loamy

East Barsham Manor

smells of the damp churchyard wafting in. A little statue of Our Lady of Walsingham sits in a niche beside a window.

Pre-Reformation, this church was under the care of the monks at Castle Acre. Next to it stood the chapel of St Saviour of the Greeting [Annunciation] of Our Lady, where pilgrims attended Mass before continuing to the Slipper Chapel, now the Catholic National Shrine to Our Lady of Walsingham, and on over the Holy Mile to Walsingham.

Next door to the church is the *Barsham Arms*, and beyond that the handsome manor house, its highly decorative brickwork making it look like an elaborate cake in dusty orange icing. From this house, says Leonard Whatmore in his book *Highway to Walsingham*: 'Henry VIII is said to have walked to the shrine of Our Lady of Walsingham barefoot.' He did so, in 1513, to pray for his infant son by Catherine of Aragon. The child did not survive

Whatmore quotes an account of Henry VIII's barefoot pilgrimage from Sir Henry Spelman, who died in 1641 at the age of 80. He had spent his boyhood in Walsingham and later recalled: 'The common report prevailed, when I was yet a boy, that Henry VIII King of England proceeded with bare feet from Barsham to the presence of the Virgin; and having made his requests offered a necklace of outstanding value; perchance to propitiate the Saint whom he was to root out of her monastic shrine and in a short time drive into banishment.'

East Barsham to Houghton St Giles and the Slipper Chapel

From East Barsham I take to the verge along the B1105 and look out for a stile and footpath on my left that Whatmore says will take me on the old pilgrim path over the fields to North Barsham.

There is no signpost to that footpath today, and I only find it by keeping my eyes on the hedge as I trudge along the wider grass verge on the other side of the road. A blue nylon rope tied to a drain grating at the roadside, and disappearing through a gap in the hedge, turns out to mark the spot.

I fight my way through the hedge to emerge in a freshly ploughed field, over which I tramp, and reflect as I go that the weather is very normal for Norfolk: the sun burns my face while the wind flays my skin. Ahead of me, as I cross the meandering River Stiffkey via a footbridge alongside a ford, is a clutch of red roofs around the 13th-century church, another dedicated to All Saints, at North Barsham.

Depopulation from the 16th century meant such villages, and their churches,

Left: Approaching All Saints, North Barsham

Above: The Slipper Chapel, Houghton St Giles

shrank from the significant pilgrim staging points they once were. North Barsham's is the plainest of buildings, a little flint chapel with a tiny bell-housing peeking above the roof line. Once, it had a tower. Today it is closed, but its churchyard offers a point for reflection before I move on.

The Slipper Chapel, which houses the Catholic National Shrine of Our Lady of Walsingham, announces itself with the appearance through the trees of a great barn of a modern church, but just beyond it is a small wayside chapel that is the only sur-viving remnant of the ancient shrine of Walsingham still in use, dating from 1360. It marks the boundary of Walsingham's inner sanctum and is the place where medieval pilgrims removed their shoes to walk the last Holy Mile to Walsingham barefoot.

From the meadows it looks like a stumpy little flint rocket ready for blast off. It's a tiny place, and only a handful of pilgrims can shuffle at a time into its cool interior. There is a queue. I await my turn, and then slip inside a simple space, with

THE SLIPPER CHAPEL, CATHOLIC NATIONAL SHRINE

The Slipper Chapel is a remarkable survivor. Thomas Cromwell, who did such a thorough job of obliterating the Holy House just down the lane at Walsingham Priory, left it alone, and it survived to be used as a poor house, a forge, a cowshed and a barn. An 1894 photograph shows cattle grazing peacefully outside.

Then it was rescued. In 1895, Charlotte Pearson Boyd bought the building and had it converted back to ecclesiastical use, giving it to the Catholic Church. In 1934 the Slipper Chapel was designated the National Shrine of Our Lady for Roman Catholics in England. After a gap of over 350 years, Walsingham was once again a place of Catholic pilgrimage.

Whatmore notes that its dedication to St Catherine of Alexandria 'is a confirmation of the persistent tradition connecting with pilgrims, since it was the Knights of St Katharine who once guarded the road to Nazareth and the Holy House, a replica of which was the centre of the Walsingham Devotion.'

This is the same saint venerated at the Royal Foundation of St Katharine, which I visited just a couple of miles into the first stage of my pilgrimage.

its white walls and terracotta floor. To the left of the altar is the statue of Our Lady (**right**), modelled on the image taken from an ancient wax seal of Walsingham Priory, and the only representation of the original shrine statue to have survived the Reformation. Mary is seated on a throne, with the child Jesus on her lap. Both wear Saxon crowns, and Mary holds a lily for a sceptre.

St Catherine has a presence here too: she is portrayed alongside the reredos with the wheel on which she was executed.

Between the modern church, modelled on a traditional Norfolk barn, and the Slipper Chapel is an area for outdoor Mass, encircled by the Stations of the Cross;

depictions of the 14 stages on Christ's final journey to his Crucifixion. To walk them is a mini-pilgrimage in itself, and I do just that.

To one side, a series of boards explain the tradition of England being offered as a Dowry to Mary (see below)

Houghton St Giles to Walsingham

I don't take my boots off for the final Holy Mile, on a permissive path that follows the track of a former railway, but I do tread softly, awed by the power of the place I am entering. The wind has dropped, and the sun is strong.

The path follows a gentle, steady gradient between embankments alive with wildflowers, under a sky full of birdsong.

ENGLAND AS OUR LADY'S DOWRY

Such was the deep devotion to Mary in medieval England, and the belief that she was the country's protector, that by the 14th century the country was regarded as Mary's Dowry: the land and its people entrusted to her guardianship.

The first recorded dedication came in 1381 when, following the Peasants' Revolt, Richard II made the proclamation: 'This is your dowry, o pious Virgin Mary'.

A small 1395 painting on two hinged wooden panels called the Wilton Diptych – now in the National Gallery – shows Richard II kneeling before the Virgin and Child. Nearby, an angel carries the Cross of St George, surmounted by an orb featuring a map of England.

Numerous shrines to Mary were established around the country, the first at Evesham in 700. Marian shrines were established at Tewkesbury and Coventry before Walsingham's in 1061, and over 30 more followed.

Their destruction was relished by Cromwell and his supporters. In 1538, his compatriot Hugh Latimer wrote to him: 'the doll of Islington [another shrine], with her older sister of Walsingham, her younger sister of Ipswich, and her two other sisters of Doncaster and Penrhys, would make a jolly muster... they would not be all day burning.'

I hear the greater whitethroat, a little brown warbler that winters in Africa, Arabia and Pakistan. Quite a pilgrim journey. Then comes the European goldfinch, with its flashes of yellow and black, and a red face with black eye patches as if it is at a masked ball. It's a bird which I have often tried, and failed, to tempt into my London garden.

As I reach Walsingham, history resonates so. At the point where I turn right to reach the road into the village, the pasture ahead of me is called Martyrs Field in memory of two local men hanged here for opposing the desecration of the Holy House (see box Langham Madonna p20).

Leonard Whatmore writes: 'the change of religion, involving as it did the destruction of Walsingham's chief *raison d'etre*, was not popular... Officially, since they rose against the despotism of Henry VIII, they may have been "traitors". By the people of the place, however, even if they might not qualify for the altar according to the canonical requirements of the church, they were regarded otherwise.'

Walsingham really does feel like a holy village – as well as being lovely, with its honeyed stone. Nowhere else in England comes as close to offering a pilgrim destination akin to Santiago de Compostela or Lourdes, as Walsingham does. Alongside the two main – Catholic and Anglican – shrines with their extensive pilgrim hostelries, it has two parish churches, a Methodist chapel, an Orthodox shrine, and is home to at least eight other religious orders. The newest is the Community of Our Lady of Walsingham, with their bright blue habits, who run Dowry House, a retreat centre.

Everywhere, fractured pilgrim history has been repaired. As I join High St I pass the ruins of a 14th-century Franciscan friary. These Greyfriars, who set up in the pilgrim trade in competition with the Augustinians at the Priory, left along with them in 1538, but returned in 2018. Three friars now serve the Catholic shrine and its pilgrims.

Walsingham Abbey

Halfway down the High St stands the still majestic gateway to the 11th century Priory of Our Lady of Walsingham, now called Walsingham Abbey. A grille in the door gives a perspective through the trees

Above – Walsingham: Orthodox Shrine (**left**) and Church of the Annunciation (**right**).

Walsingham Abbey: Gateway (**above**) and ruins of the Holy House of Nazareth (**below**).

HISTORY OF THE HOLY HOUSE

The Holy House was built in 1061 and made of wood. In the 1500s, however, a stone chapel was carefully wrapped around the original. An account by Erasmus, the Renaissance scholar and Christian philosopher who came on pilgrimage from Cambridge, gives us a very clear picture of what pilgrims found here.

Within the stone chapel, he writes, 'there is a small chapel built on a wooden platform. Pilgrims are admitted through a narrow door on each side. There is very little light: only what comes from tapers, which have a most pleasing scent... and if you peer inside... you would say it was the abode of saints, so dazzling is it with jewels, gold, and silver'.

Of the statue of Virgin and Child, he writes: 'there was a dim religious light, and she stood in the shadows to the right of the altar... a small image... unimpressive in size, material and workmanship but of surpassing power.'

Erasmus says that pilgrims visited other points in the abbey, including holy wells. On the altar of the priory church was a crystal phial said to contain Mary's sacred milk.

A contemporary ballad, *The Walsingham Lament*, expressed the sense of loss at the Dissolution:

'Weepe, weepe O Walsingham,
whose days are nightes,
Blessings turn to blasphemies,
holy deeds to dispites.'

Right: Walsingham Anglican Shrine

to the soaring arch that once framed the east window of the abbey church. I pop round the corner to enter via the Shirehall, a pilgrim hostel in the 15th century, and pass through a belt of trees to reach a glade in which the ruined priory stands.

The greatest surviving element is that soaring gothic arch, defying gravity and its desecrators to frame the tranquil Norfolk countryside. A modest little board marks the place where the shrine of the Holy House of Nazareth once stood. Not a scrap of it was spared, an indication of the fear its power instilled in Henry VIII and Cromwell.

Two entries in the priory accounts for 1538 pinpoint the catastrophe. Those for Lady Day, March 25, show that Henry VIII made his usual payment for the prior's salary, for a candle to be kept burning at the shrine, and for a priest to sing. When the Michaelmas payments came due on September 29, the entry reads: 'For the king's candle before Our Lady of Walsingham, and to the prior there for his salary, nil.'

It was the end.

The Anglican Shrine of Our Lady of Walsingham

Around the corner in Holt Rd is the Anglican Shrine of Our Lady of Walsingham, set within a glorious walled garden. It was built in the 1930s, so has no intrinsic history of its own, but enter and you find at its heart a remarkable

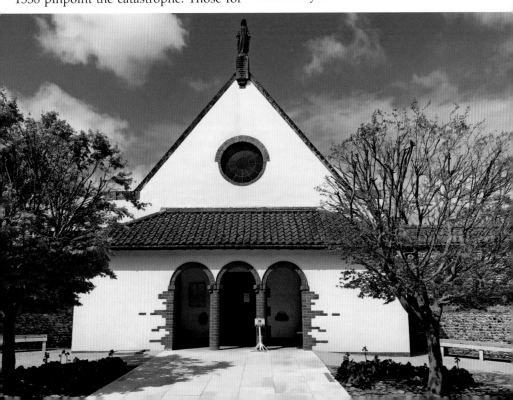

modern replica of the original Holy House.

This is a quite astounding place. I have never been anywhere so ornate, so richly decorated, so – in a word – Catholic. Such is the contrast to the simplicity of the Slipper Chapel that I wonder for a moment if I haven't got my Anglican and Catholic shrines transposed.

With its gold, jewels and deep lustrous colours the shrine church emulates the richness of the original Holy House and becomes a powerful sensory link to it. It is truly awe-inspiring, and I walk around it once in amazement, unable to separate the kaleidoscope of images that bombard me: a fragment of the true cross in a golden reliquary; the pierced feet of Jesus disappearing through the ceiling as he ascends to heaven; a statue of Richeldis in a gold cloak and blue dress, holding a replica of the original, simple Holy House in her hand.

During building work, a minor miracle occurred: they discovered a well (**right**), producing a steady flow of

pure, clear water, and it was incorporated into the church. I reach it below ground, down steps beneath a brick arch, where it is covered with a glass disc and is watched over by a gold statue of Our Lady of Walsingham. Pilgrims drink, and are sprinkled with, its waters.

Beside it is a memorial tomb to Fr Alfred Hope Patten, the Anglican vicar of

Walsingham, who drove the re-creation of this shrine and whose great friend, Fr Henry Fynes Clinton, supported his efforts and created a shrine to Our Lady of Walsingham in his church of St Magnus the Martyr, where my pilgrimage began, 177.9 miles away.

Finally, I come to the replica of the original Holy House, enclosed within the shrine church, and a very theatrical space. It has no windows, and is lit solely by the hundreds of candles, burning here to mark the intentions, sent in from parishes all over the world, that line the walls.

All is darkness beyond these pinpricks of light, and the eye is drawn to the gold and piercing blue of the altar, above which a replica of the original statue of Our Lady of Walsingham shimmers in her finery, as if picked out by a spotlight.

I have arrived in time for Shrine Prayers and soak up one of the most remarkable services I have ever experienced. Fr Ben Bradshaw, the shrine priest, addresses us as 'Dear friends and fellow pilgrims'. Shrine Prayers takes the form of praying the Rosary, today focusing on the Sorrowful Mysteries on Christ's path to His Crucifixion. Built around the prayers are a whole string of intercessions.

There are dozens and dozens of prayers: for named individuals including Fr Hope Patten, for churches, for care homes, for the departed, for those anxious about loved ones, for those seeking reconciliation, for spiritual health. Finally, Fr Ben addresses Mary directly: 'You are our mother, our life, our sweetness and our hope.'

My London to Walsingham Camino has been a remarkable journey. I feel as if my one set of footprints have left the very faintest of tracks here, all the way from London. Later, as I sit in the shrine's peaceful garden, I imagine other footsteps joining mine, a few at first, then more and more until the path of the London to Walsingham Camino is a wide and clear one. One that is waymarked and established as a true Camino. One of a web of routes leading to England's remarkable Marian shrine, from Norwich, Ely, Kings Lynn and elsewhere.

Below: The Holy House, Anglican Shrine

INDEX

NOTE **bold** = photo